THE MAGIAN TAROK

"Every occultist of whatever stripe has at least one tarot deck. Most of them have either no clue as to origins or, worse still, have bought into bad eighteenth- or nineteenth-century pseudo-mythology. The deeper roots in Roman and Persian symbols are well traced here by Stephen E. Flowers, who is both a practicing magician and a respected scholar of Indo-European religions and languages. This book is a wondrous blend of scholarship (into areas not available in English or even German or French) and deeply insightful practice of Hermeticism. For the powerful human who knows the age-old secret, 'To master the Fruit, know ye the Root.' This volume is essential reading both for the tarot and for understanding the Persian contribution to modern occultism."

DON WEBB, AUTHOR OF
OVERTHROWING THE OLD GODS

"Like every book penned by Stephen E. Flowers, this too is an epitome of erudite readability and is proof positive of his uncanny knack of digging up the most enlightening arcane information— enticing and surprising lay readers and experts alike. The deep tarot as you've never known it, highly recommended!"

FRATER U∴D∴, FOUNDER OF PRAGMATIC AND ICE MAGIC
AND AUTHOR OF *THE MAGICAL SHIELD* AND *SEX MAGIC*

"For many years Stephen E. Flowers, Ph.D., has pushed the boundaries of Western esoteric discourse by introducing obscure untranslated texts and authors to English-language audiences. His concise and approachable analysis of Sigurd Agrell's tarot theories has once again opened the way for scholarship on an otherwise ignored topic, and *The Magian Tarok* is sure to be the definitive reference on its subject for years to come."

STUART SÜDEKUM, TAROT INSTRUCTOR

THE MAGIAN TAROK

The Origins of the Tarot in the Mithraic and Hermetic Traditions

STEPHEN E. FLOWERS, PH.D.

Third Revised and Expanded Edition

Inner Traditions
Rochester, Vermont

Inner Traditions
One Park Street
Rochester, Vermont 05767
www.InnerTraditions.com

Text stock is SFI certified

Originally published in 2006 by Runa-Raven Press under the title *The Magian Tarok: The Key Linking the Mithraic, Greek, Roman, Hebrew and Tunic Traditions of the Tarot*
Second edition published in 2015 by Lodestar Books
Third revised and expanded edition published in 2019 by Inner Traditions

Cataloging-in-Publication Data for this title is available from the Library of Congress

ISBN 978-1-62055-869-0 (print)
ISBN 978-1-62055-870-6 (ebook)

Printed and bound in the United States by Lake Book Manufacturing, Inc. The text stock is SFI certified. The Sustainable Forestry Initiative® program promotes sustainable forest management.

10 9 8 7 6 5 4 3 2 1

Text design and layout by Debbie Glogover
This book was typeset in Garamond Premier Pro with Brioso Pro, Goudy OldStyle Std, and Gill Sans MT Pro used as display typefaces

To send correspondence to the author of this book, mail a first-class letter to the author c/o Inner Traditions • Bear & Company, One Park Street, Rochester, VT 05767, and we will forward the communication, or contact the author directly at **runa@texas.net**.

ACKNOWLEDGMENTS

I would like to thank Don Webb for his suggestions regarding the original draft of the manuscript for this book. I also wish to thank the late Daniel Young for his thoughtful reading of the original manuscript. Michael Moynihan, Jon Graham, Paul Huson, Stuart Südekum, and Oldřich Hrabanek each contributed something special to the contents of this book.

Abbreviations

Av.	Avestan
BCE	Before the Common Era (= B.C. = Before Christ)
CE	Common Era (= A.D. = Anno Domini)
ch.	chapter
Copt.	Coptic
Egypt.	Egyptian
Ger.	German
Gk.	Greek
Heb.	Hebrew
Lat.	Latin
Pers.	Persian
PGM	Standard reference to the Greek magical papyri edited by Preisendanz
pl.	plural
RV	*Rig Veda*
sg.	singular

A Note on Terminology

The terms *Mithra, Mithrist,* and *Mithrism* are used in this book when reference is being made to the cult of Mithra in the ancient Iranian world. In discussions of the later mystery cult of the Greco-Roman classical world, the terms *Mithras, Mithraist,* and *Mithraism* are used.

CONTENTS

Origins Shrouded in Mystery

No part of the modern occult revival has held more general fascination than the tarot. Whole novels have been based on its symbolism, and hundreds of books written and published. There are no fewer than two hundred commercially printed tarot decks on the market—from a facsimile of the oldest nearly complete set (the Visconti-Sforza) to innovative and even fanciful versions such as the "Tarot of the Cat People" or the "Native American Tarot." This unfortunate process of modernization and desacralization has gone so far that one can even now buy "Teen Tarot" packages.

Such general fascination must ultimately stem from some deep-seated, archetypal validity. But the true source of this archetype has eluded, or has seemed to elude, most researchers. The deepest origins of the tarot have remained shrouded in mystery.

In this book, by using the postmodern methods outlined in my previous study titled *Hermetic Magic,* I explore for the first time for a lay readership the historical roots of the symbolism of the Major Arcana of the tarot. Many of the "myths" surrounding the cards will be confirmed—for example, there is indeed a deep-level connection with Egypt, with the Roma, and with the Semitic tradition. But these connections are only the tip of a greater iceberg. What for centuries has been lying below the surface of these myths has the potential for opening the understanding of the tarot to previously unknown levels of power.

I first got the idea for this book in 1981 when I was doing research in Germany. There I found many texts on the subject of magic in academic libraries. I have often remarked to students that the true occult literature of our time is not to be found in the occult section of our bookstores but rather in the halls of academia. The resources that lie there are often really hidden. Professors and doctoral candidates work for years on ideas. They research, document, and eventually publish them. But the finished product appears in obscure journals or even more obscure proceedings of conferences. Often they remain unread even by specialists in the field. And as often as not the significance of such works remains hidden—not only from the public but also even from the conscious minds of those who wrote them.

The groundbreaking research for this work was published in the 1930s by a Swedish philologist and professor named Sigurd Agrell (1885–1937). His single most important work for the object of this book is *Die pergamenische Zauberscheibe und das Tarockspiel* (The Magical Disk of Pergamon and the Game of Tarot), published in 1936. Agrell is perhaps better known for his somewhat controversial work in the field of runology. He published a series of works in the 1920s and 1930s showing a link between Mithraic cult practices and beliefs and the tradition of the older Germanic runes. This pursuit led him to study the symbolism of the tarot as well as that of Lappish shamans. Because certain technical details of his runological theories (i.e., his famous Uthark theory) were generally rejected by contemporary scholars, other aspects of his work, and legitimate dimensions within it, have often been unfairly ignored. With this study I take a fresh look at some of Agrell's data and bring it up to date with many new perspectives.

This is not a book about divinatory practices using the tarot, although knowledge gained from these pages can certainly enhance the *insight* necessary for divination utilizing the tarot. Neither is it a textbook for a new deck of tarot cards—although it is my hope that someone will use the contents of this book to redesign a deck and thereby restore the original *mysteria,* or dare I say *râzân,* attendant to the icons. The card images created by Amber Rae Broderick that appear in each of the Major Arcana are examples of the power such a pursuit can bring. Even if the ultimate theory upon which Agrell's work was based cannot be proved, his studies can certainly be seen to illuminate the symbolism of the tarot with a new light and may lead to more discoveries.

The text of the original version of this book was substantially finished in 1992 and appeared in a preliminary edition but was not published more widely until a second edition was produced in 2006. This third edition is vastly expanded and improved with not only new material but also a revision of some of the systemic errors in the original edition, stemming from limited understanding of the Iranian tradition.

The chief aim of this work is to demonstrate a method for arriving at symbols for personal transformation based on the discovery of hidden, deep-level correspondences. This book does not represent a grand conclusion of a process but rather the first—or second—step in a journey of rediscovery of the deeper roots of a significant part of the Western tradition.

Stephen E. Flowers,
Woodharrow, 2019

THE MAGIAN TAROT
AND POSTMODERN THEORY

Many philosophers and historians of culture have come to the conclusion that the Western world is entering upon a new epoch of history. The changes that are sweeping the Westernized cultures are similar to those that swept across it with the coming of Christianity and the onset of the Middle Ages (in the early part of the first millennium CE) or the triumph of Scientism following the Renaissance (around 1500 CE). This later development led to what we call the Modern world today.

More recent changes, mainly in the late-twentieth century, have laid the groundwork for another epochal change, another paradigm shift. Worlds come to an end, and worlds are generated, constantly. "Bubba theologians" who watch the skies for signs of the coming apocalypse are wasting their time grasping at shadows. The apocalypse is actually an ongoing phenomenon. In fact, we are in the midst of a major apocalyptic event at every *present moment in history.*

Changes that occurred in the Western world over the last half of the twentieth century point to an epochal shift. One of the current names for this shift is "postmodernism." Postmodernism is characterized by freedom from the oppressive modern myth of progress—the idea

1

that as time goes on, by applying ever increasing amounts of rationality and scientific methodology, the problems of the world will universally evaporate in the light of pure reason. Postmodernists realize, as did the ancients, that such progress is only possible for individuals—through *initiation.*

To the modernist, if something is not new, not the latest thing, then it is retrograde or reactionary, and hence inferior and perhaps unacceptable. True postmodernists are free of these constraints of modern progressiveness. Postmodernists freely synthesize elements from every phase of human history. For this reason, bodies of lore, such as that represented by the tarot, gain a new relevance and potential for the development of the individual.

Postmodernism is a general school of cultural thought that has been growing in Western European societies since the end of the Second World War. No premise of postmodernism is more important than the abandonment of the "myth of progress" based on the cooperative, monolithic application of scientific rationalism. The events of the twentieth century demonstrated that, despite a quantum leap in science and technology, the human species, if it had changed at all, had only become worse. Quantum leaps in rationality, education, and practical applications of science had not equaled even a moderate amount of true human progress in any spiritual sense. Modernism had proved itself, at least to some, to be a failed experiment.

Unfortunately, the whole idea of postmodernism has generally been hijacked by Marxists and crypto-Marxists, especially in the American academy. Marxism itself is a quintessential school of modernism, but as it lost its worldwide position of prestige in the wake of the general failure of Marxist states at the dawn of the 1990s, its theories were retooled and weaponized as the doctrines of "po-mo," as some like to call it. This movement has become established in the American academy from the highest levels down to kindergarten. This version of postmodernism should not confuse the reader. Ignore it, if you can.

An essential component of the general, non-Marxist, postmodern theory is the realization that myth represents a higher reality. Myth determines reality, and modifications in mythology can cause alterations in perceived reality. Modernists were simply dreaming in a self-created delusion when they posited the idea that mythology would be superseded by science or that mythology could even be comprehensively described by science. Today's world is dominated by science, yet myths and the suprarational—and even the surreal—abound. To be sure, much of it is of the lowest quality, as will quickly be found on the many sorts of platforms of digital misinformation that exist today. But in fact, at the present the appetite for the mythic and the mysterious only seems to grow with the average person's level of education. Modernism has failed to provide symbolic meaning for people's lives—and without deep symbolic meaning, a culture cannot long survive.

With the rejection of the idea that progress and rationalism are in and of themselves valuable things, postmodernists are open to explore the validity of past models or paradigms. Past—or perhaps better stated, eternal—models of human understanding are seen with new eyes. Their value is perceived as something more than just historical curiosities with their relevance to the future limited to their roles as past foundations. Also, legitimate approaches to these paradigms are liberated from the purely rationalistic mode. The present academic sciences will become obsolete by their limited natures when it comes to unraveling the mysteries they were originally designed to explain.

Essential to the postmodern theory of magic is the idea of *communication*. Postmodern theory might also be called a *semiotic* theory of mythology and magic. Semiotics is the study of signs and symbols—the theory and practice of how meaning is conveyed from a sender to a receiver and back again. When these things happen, communication takes place. This process is not without mysterious components, as becomes apparent even when considering the most mundane conversation between two human beings. Science cannot answer the most basic and essential questions concerning the nature of the sender and receiver (their psyches) or of the system they use to communicate (language). What is it? Where did it come from? How does it work? It has been said by the wisest of men that nothing that has its origins in the human mind can be reduced to a set of logical, rational rules. The soul is not a compilation of chemical reactions—otherwise its mysteries would have long since been unraveled.

When considering semiotics in the theory of operative magic, I wrote in *Hermetic Magic:*

> The semiotic theory of magic states that magic is a process of inter-reality communication—when, in Hermetic terms, that which is below is able to communicate its will to that which is above and thereby bring about a modification in the configuration of that which is above (the subtle paradigms of the cosmos) and thereby receive a return message in the form of corresponding modifications in the environment "below." That this should be so is not rational or natural, it is not subject to objective experimentation—it is a non-natural (rather than "supernatural") event. To be sure, magical communication does not take place in exactly the same form as mundane communication, but it does follow the analogous archetypal principles.[1]

These principles are just as much at work when we consider the possibilities of illustrative or illuminative workings of mythology. Systems such as the tarot are mythic maps of the world and of consciousness. They represent a means for "inter-reality communication," and give insight into the encoding system within the sender of the mysterious communications. This amounts to being able to know the mind of a god.

If it is indeed the search for meaningfulness that most drives the souls of individual human beings, then it is essential that there be a metalanguage of signs and symbols in which such meaningfulness can be communicated precisely. The tarot can be seen to represent such a system.

Our task in this study is to open the underlying mythology of the tarot to its historical roots and thereby expand its frame of reference beyond the Judeo-Christian confines into which it was forced in the years following the Renaissance.

Shifting the paradigm upon which the tarot system is based from a Judeo-Christian one back to its original syncretic pagan roots represents more than just creating another imaginative tarot mythology. It is rooted in objective data and is essentially a movement away from the medieval basis of the modern myth of universal salvation, back toward the eternal myth of individual salvation through initiation. By shifting the myths upon which the world is based, we shift the basis of reality. The power to do so belongs to the ones who control the pole of reality around which all things revolve.

As we will discover, the Magians of two thousand years ago were in a position very similar to the one in which postmodern magicians find themselves today—a maelstrom of cultural influences in a world of ever-shifting values and mental patterns. Their active response to it and the response of the postmodernists to our times can be seen to have much in common, at least potentially.

CHAPTER I

A Modern History
of the Tarot

For two hundred years occult scholars have been fascinated with the tarot and have connected the symbolism of the Major Arcana (or Trumps) to a diverse set of mystical sources and meanings. What lies before you is a key to unlocking the actual sources of tarot symbolism as it historically developed from the very earliest times. This key to understanding is one that takes into account how these sources work together *Hermetically.*

The most widespread and popular myths about the tarot surround its supposed origins in ancient Egypt. Many older writers (and some modern ones) make claims about the original Egyptian symbolism—that subterranean initiatory chambers were lined with the tarot images, and so on. Another quite old myth is that the tarot has some original connection with the so-called Gypsies. The first myth and the second are closely connected in the minds of European Christians. When the Romani people arrived in Europe during the sixteenth century, they were identified by various Europeans as being Egyptians (hence the nickname Gypsies). The reason for this was that any exotic, "heathen" people from the East were identified by ignorant Christian Europeans with the exotic heathens depicted in what was perhaps the only book of history and ethnography they knew: the Bible. In fact, the origins of the Romani people have nothing whatsoever to do with Egypt. They speak a language (Romani, also spelled Romany) that belongs to the Dardic family of Indo-Iranian, closely akin to the dialects spoken in Kashmir and in what is modern northern Pakistan. These people migrated westward from their central Asiatic homeland beginning more than a thousand years ago and by the 1500s were found throughout Europe.

A Persian legend about the origin of the Romani is found in an epic Persian poem, the *Shahnameh* of Firdowsi. It states that the Sasanian emperor Bahrām V Gōr discovered that the poor could not afford to enjoy music. Therefore, he requested that the king of India send ten thousand *luris,* male and female lute-playing musicians, to Persia. When the musicians arrived, the shah gave each one an ox and a donkey and a supply of wheat so that they would be able to live by farming and provide free musical entertainment to the poor of Persia. But it is said that the musicians ate the oxen and the wheat and were starving after a year had passed. The shah was angry that they had wasted what he had given them and commanded that that they be exiled to wander around the world. The original religion of the Romani is said to have been a form of Hinduism. In any case, this legend shows that it is likely that the Romani spent some time in the Persian Empire before immigrating to Europe. It is likely that they absorbed Iranian ideas into their Indic mythology. (Most Romani today are professed Christians.)

A third myth surrounding the tarot is that it has some original connection with the Hebrew Kabbalah. The genesis of this myth lies with the origin of occult interest in the tarot at the end of the eighteenth and the beginning of the nineteenth centuries. With a certain limited kind of logic, occult scholars reasoned that if there were twenty-two Major Arcana, and twenty-two Hebrew letters—the elements of foundation— there must be some connection. Writers such as Éliphas Lévi and Papus pursued this vigorously and set the tone for what was to become the Western occult tradition surrounding the tarot.

All of these myths may be seen to have more than a grain of truth in them, but each is equally misleading in its own way. In what follows

I explore the objective history of the tarot and show the genesis of its symbolism in the great Hermetic tradition of the early part of this era—roughly at the same time as the magical papyri were being written. What will emerge is a new picture of the tarot, more closely linked with pre- and non-Judeo-Christian traditions and most especially with the Mithraic or Magian (Iranian) tradition.

Throughout this study my chief guidelines have been provided by the work of the Swedish scholar Sigurd Agrell, who wrote most of his academic works in the 1920s and 1930s. But I will also go beyond what Agrell has suggested, based on more recent scholarship in the areas of the tarot as well as Mithraism and the history of ancient Iranian religions.

Cards such as the now well-known tarot cards were used in some sort of game playing in the late Middle Ages. Such artifacts were unknown before the fourteenth century. The earliest reference to such cards is in a decree of the city of Florence in 1376.

The oldest tarot images, in the form of hand-painted cards, date from the fifteenth century. At this earliest time, Italy was the region where most of the cards were produced and used. Beyond Italy they were

Sigurd Agrell (1881–1937)

most often found in other Romance regions, especially in France. No one can say for sure when or where the tarot images originated, only that the oldest examples come from that time and place. The original name, *tarocco* (pl. *tarocchi*), is also Italian, although the derivation of the word is debated. The form of the word normally used in modern English is from the French *tarot* [tar-OH], or [tar-OTT] in the medieval pronunciation. Some modern occultists like to connect the word with the Hebrew Torah, the Law, and often make the claim that the iconic tarot was revealed to Moses in Egypt and provided the structure for an esoteric side of the exoteric Law revealed to the Law-Giver on Sinai.

The oldest actual tarot cards in existence were fashioned in Italy during the early fifteenth century. Certainly the tradition of the cards must go back some time before that. A historical record from 1392 indicates that Jacquemin Gringonneur created a set of gilded cards for King Charles IV of France. These are thought by some to survive as an incomplete set of seventeen cards now preserved in the Bibliothèque Nationale in Paris. From the art-historical evidence, however, it seems that these cards are actually of fifteenth-century Venetian origin. The images on these and other isolated early cards of the tarot type often give keys to understanding the origin of the tarot. In this earliest period of existing tarot representation, archaic variations survive that are later leveled out, or regularized, by certain esoteric dogmas in subsequent eras.

The oldest verified tarot images also come from Italy: the Visconti-Sforza Tarot of the fifteenth century. These were probably created in the court of the Sforza family, which ruled in Milan in northern Italy from 1450 to 1535. These too demonstrate variations in the standard imagery associated with the Major Arcana. This is because most modern occult revival decks are specifically derived from the Marseilles deck, which dates from the eighteenth century. It was this set of designs that was used as a basis of the speculations of Éliphas Lévi and, later, S. L. MacGregor Mathers. Others, using these speculations as a basis, began to create new versions of the cards based on the archetype provided by the Marseilles deck.

Conservatively, we must say that the tarot, as a complete and fixed symbol system, could not have originated before the fifteenth century. However, there may have been an older systematic archetype upon which the tarot system was ultimately based. It is equally hard to believe that the system was simply invented out of whole cloth in Renaissance Italy. This would be virtually impossible in a world where tradition and authority were valued beyond any mere whimsical originality. The most conservative interpretation would be that they were invented, but by making use of Hermetic, Neoplatonic, and other esoteric speculations current in northern Italy during the Renaissance. A deeper look might take into account the more archaic lore surrounding the letters of the Roman and Greek alphabets and their connections with Mithraic ideas current in late antiquity.

The source for the associations between the twenty-two tarot cards and the oracular use of the twenty-two letters of the Roman (Latin) alphabet appears to have been lost. But many more sources were known to the Renaissance Hermetics than have survived. For the Italians, the association between the Roman alphabet and the mysterious icons may also have been too ordinary and domestic to excite much in the way of wondrous awe. It is most likely that the system was shaped and fixed, and only later endowed with a myth of primordial tradition. At that point, it becomes pointless to search for any other source.

THE MODERN ESOTERIC TAROT

Speculations such as the one about the esoteric side of the tarot stem from the general occult revival of the late eighteenth and early nineteenth centuries. It was French occultists in particular who led the way in such speculations concerning the tarot. Court de Gebelin, in his book *Le monde primitif* (1781), seems to have coined the title "The Book of Thoth" for the tarot and to have promoted the idea that the symbols were of Egyptian origin. Alliette, a well-known French wigmaker (or algebra professor, depending on who tells the story), who went by the pseudonym Etteilla, made his reputation using the tarot for divinatory purposes. He was also the first to try to bring the tarot, astrology, and the Kabbalah into one whole system. But his efforts were rather superficial.

By the middle of the nineteenth century writers such as Éliphas Lévi (Alphonse Louis Constant, 1810–1875) and Papus (Gérard Encausse, 1865–1916) had fully encoded the tarot symbolism into that of the Hebrew Kabbalah—which had in modern times become the most common framework of Western esotericism. In 1856, Lévi was the first writer to ascribe the value of the Hebrew letters to the Major Arcana directly, and thus to ascribe the cards to the Tree of Life model. He did this in his landmark book, *Le Dogme et Rituel de la Haute Magie* (Transcendental Magic).

It is known that Lévi had some contact with the English order known as the Societas Rosicruciana in Anglia, some of the members of which were involved in the foundation of the Hermetic Order of the Golden Dawn in 1888.

After Lévi's death in 1875, other French occultists continued his work. In 1889 both Papus and Oswald Wirth, a disciple of Marquis Stanislas de Guaita, published esoteric studies on the tarot.

In Great Britain, Samuel Liddell MacGregor Mathers (1854–1918) codified knowledge of the tarot into the system of the Hermetic Order of the Golden Dawn. In this order initiates were instructed to create their own tarot cards based on verbal instructions. Mathers's main structural contribution to the esoteric tarot was his enumeration of The Fool as 0.

Shortly after 1900 the Hermetic Order of the Golden Dawn entered in a series of schisms and name changes that also brought about several splinter groups. One member of the original temple who retained a position of authority in it was Arthur Edward Waite (1857–1942). Waite gradually influenced a series of reforms toward a more mystical direction in preparation for a coup, which finally occurred in 1909 when he seized full control of the organization, rejecting the practice of ceremonial magic and the trappings of ahistorical Egyptian paraphernalia that had been present up to that point. Waite's new version of the order was called the Independent & Rectified Rite of the Golden Dawn. In the place of pseudo-Egyptian magic, Waite substituted Platonic mysticism from the Western tradition (or "Secret Tradition," as Waite termed it). In collaboration with the artist Pamela Colman Smith, Waite created his rectified tarot, which was intended as a contemplative tool expressing the underlying symbolism that united the Christian and pre-Christian eras. In 1909 the Rider Company produced Waite's tarot deck along with a book of his commentary titled *The Key to the Tarot.* In 1910, Rider published a revised and expanded version of Waite's text as *The Pictorial Key to the Tarot.* The tarot cards that Waite designed have since become known as the Rider-Waite deck. This set of images made two chief contributions to the history of the tarot. The first has to do with the international popularity the deck achieved. The second, and probably the reason for this popularity, is the fact that for the first time the Minor Arcana too were given pictorial images. Before this innovation the Minor Arcana, which originally may have had nothing to do with the series of images called the Major Arcana, were represented only with schematic arrangements of numbers of wands, swords, cups, or disks. It should also be noted that Waite, for whatever reasons, reversed the order of Justice (VIII) and Strength (XI).

The origin of the pictorial symbolism of the Minor Arcana is traceable to the meanings of the suit and court cards of the normal deck of playing cards, as they themselves were used in fortune-telling as early as the fifteenth century. Our modern tarot deck appears to be a combination of the Major Arcana and normal playing cards as used for divinatory purposes in Europe.

Playing cards as such are a cultural phenomenon dependent upon the invention of the printing press. The first playing cards were used in China in the ninth century CE. The idea of playing cards spread along the Silk Road into Persia and the rest of the Islamic world. The final form of the familiar deck of playing cards we use today, and with which the images that made up the Arcana were combined to make the tarot deck, took shape in the Islamic world under significant Persian influence in the twelfth to thirteenth centuries. The suits and court cards are seen to have originated in conjunction with Persian ideas of court culture that predate Islam. Paul Huson outlines this theory in his book *The Mystical Origins of the Tarot*.[1] According to this theory, the four suits are based on the four classes of ancient Persian society: priests, kings/warriors, farmers/craftsmen, and service people (paid workers). If this is true, as it appears to be, then here we have one more example of how this whole system was, at its earliest stages of development, a reflection of the Iranian world. This analysis is doubly interesting since the French philologist Georges Dumézil first based his groundbreaking tripartite theory of archaic Indo-European religion and culture upon similar Iranian evidence.

After the innovations of Waite, the most significant contribution to the modern popularization of the tarot came from Aleister Crowley (1875–1947). His major book on the subject, *The Book of Thoth* (1944), coincided with a new set of tarot images, which Crowley created in collaboration with the artist Lady Frieda Harris. The book appeared in a small edition and only became widely influential when it was reissued several decades after Crowley's death. Crowley too could not resist tampering with the modern tradition just a bit. His main innovations came in the renaming of many of the Major Arcana; for example, Strength became Lust, Temperance became Art, and The Last Judgment became Aeon. These and other innovations were done in the interest of tailoring the system to his own Thelemite philosophy.

Such modern occult traditions have proved to be artful and in some cases have led to profound levels of inspiration and creative activity. But in retrospect they seem to have been somewhat arbitrary attempts to reconcile modern and medieval belief systems with little to no knowledge of the roots of actual ancient traditions. It is important to remember that much of what has been given the aura of antiquity by modern occult writers is actually of relatively recent origin. This realization frees us to consider elements of the tradition that go against what has become the standard modern interpretations of the icons. For this book, the general research position is that of going deeper into more distant roots of ideas and images, to delve beyond the limitations imposed by modern (post–1500 CE) writers.

More objective and less sentimental, but nevertheless sympathetic, research shows that the tarot is most likely related to the same body of material as that of the magical papyri of the first to fifth centuries CE and the rest of the oldest Hermetic tradition. The most archaic roots of this lore may be found in the diverse sources of Indo-Iranian religion and magic, as well as that of the Mesopotamians and Egyptians. One of the first grand syntheses of these traditions was likely made in the mid–first century BCE in the Persian Empire—the home of the first martial cult of Mithra and the land of the ancient Magian priesthood. This is a body of material that also affected the early development of traditions such as the Kabbalah and alchemy. The tarot seems to be most firmly a part of a specifically Mithraic aspect of what generally came to be called the Hermetic synthesis. This was, at least, the seed idea of Sigurd Agrell.

CHAPTER 2

MAGIANISM AND
MITHRISM/MITHRAISM

O ur purpose is to unlock the deepest levels of the imagery of the tarok (tarot). To do this, we will have to delve back deeply into the root levels of the mythology and lore of the Iranian world and to two of its reflections: one known as Magianism and the other as Mithrism. Both of these systems are branches of the greater Iranian cultural and ideological sphere. In turn, this Iranian mythic system is a part of the older Indo-Iranian culture. This culture is ultimately derived from the even more archaic and larger Indo-European world—to which most European cultures and linguistic groups (e.g., the Germanic, Celtic, Slavic, Italic, and Hellenic [Greek]) also belong. This common Indo-European root accounts for many of the similarities we find between the ancient Iranian and Indian mythology on the one hand, and the Germanic, Celtic, Roman, and Greek on the other.

Originally the Iranian religious cult was almost identical to the Vedic one (such as was later recorded in India in the *Rig Veda*). Sacrifices were made to gods of royalty, war, and fertility for long life and prosperity. In the Iranian world, originally situated far to the north and east of present-day Iran, about 1700 BCE there lived a priest of this cult named Zarathustra. He saw the excesses and abuses of this cult and

15

culture: excess animal sacrifice, warriors running amok over the population, crass sorcery, and so on. In a flash of insight, Zarathustra saw that there was but one high and absolute divinity: pure, focused consciousness. He identified this deity as Ahura Mazda (Lord-Wisdom). All of the other gods and goddesses were seen as abstract principles and entities created by Ahura Mazda and which emanated from this ultimate source. This system was the first religion of the kind we know so well today: a religion in which a person could choose freely and of his or her own individual sovereign will. Zarathustra taught an ethical system of good thoughts, good words, and good actions. A brotherhood was created to pass along his teachings in the form of the poems, which he composed, called the *Gathas*. (Only a portion of these survive today, but the religion based on them still exists in the form of Zoroastrianism and is also embodied in the Mazdan Way in the West.) The brotherhood founded in Zarathustra's time became known as the Mazmaga, or the Great Fellowship. Under the guidance and leadership of this fellowship, the Persians shaped the first great world empire—the Achaemenid Empire (550–330 BCE). This empire was chiefly the vision of Cyrus the Great (598–530 BCE). The purpose of this empire was not merely political or economic but also religious in the sense that it was an attempt to cause all of the nations of the world to live in peace and prosperity.

By the time of this Achaemenid Empire, the doctrines of Zarathustran religion had already become the established, dominant philosophy and ideology of the ruling elite in the Persian Empire. But this school of thought did not coerce others to follow its doctrines precisely. Each individual had to arrive at the truth from within. Because of this, the old pre-Zoroastrian cult persisted widely and other heterodox viewpoints flourished throughout the empire. The two major streams of thought that attract our attention in this study are Magianism along with the ideology of Zurvanism, which was at times attached to Zoroastrian philosophy and Mithrism/Mithraism itself. The reasons these schools of thought are important for our work is because they are the two that were most influential in the West and in the western parts of Persia, and later in the Parthian and Sasanian Empires.

One dimension of Iranian and Zoroastrian religious history that often leads to confusion among writers is the presence of what is called the Mazmaga, or the Great Fellowship, in the deep Iranian tradition. In his lifetime the prophet Zarathustra established a school for the perpetuation of his teachings in poetic form. A remnant of his own words, first composed and recited as early as 1700 BCE, survives in the texts known today as the *Gathas*. This school of students and priests in the Good Religion (or *Mazdayasna,* "wisdom worship") have kept the flame burning, both literally and figuratively, in perpetuity. Part of what they have done historically is spread the principles of the Good Religion into other faiths when they encountered them. In the early centuries of Zoroastrianism there were massive converts to the faith, but following an ancient pattern they also had the habit of gently insinuating good traits into existing religions or mystery cults without making it known that they were the source of this. This allowed the local cult or religious reformers to take credit for the new ideas. Although generally effective, this strategy often went wrong because the underlying rationale and philosophy could be abandoned in the cult's efforts to expand and conquer others at all costs. Thus, the element of coercion was added. This is the story behind both Christianity and Islam. Some say that the Sufi movement is essentially a project of the old Mazmaga. But because of the principle of non-coercion, such movements cannot be controlled in some conspiratorial way; spiritual development has to stem from the changes wrought in individuals. This individual change, or initiation, is at the root of Mithrism/Mithraism.

Magianism can be used as a general term for the priestly practices of various tribes and cults of the Iranians from the earliest of times. Some believe that the title was originally derived from a tribal name among the Medes, an Iranian people whose empire preceded the Persians. This tribe perhaps formed a priestly class among these Medes. It may well have also been that the title was common among all Iranian peoples. In either case, the word is etymologically related to the Germanic word *mahtiz,* which gives us our word "might." Both "magic" and "might" are based on the common Indo-European root *magh-,* "to be able, to have power." So the meaning of the terms was basically and originally "one who has power," or "one who expresses power." We know that the Chinese of the eighth century BCE and the ancient Greeks and Romans all knew of the *magûs/magoi* among the Iranians. As the title was a general one, it conveys no strictly limited ideological content—only original Iranian identity. Some Magians were orthodox Zoroastrian priests, while others were members of various cult groups or sects, such as Zurvanism and perhaps Mithrism. Because all of these groups were originally part of Iranian culture, elements of Iranian thought and cultural norms inevitably dominated their founding principles. The idea of a great divine power, a pantheon of divine emanations linked to space (the stars, night sky, etc.) and time (the motion of the heavenly bodies through space fixed to a calendar) were common features.

Plutarch, writing in *Isis and Osiris* from the *Moralia* (sections 46–47), gives the following report on the religion of the magi:

> The great majority and the wisest of men hold this opinion: they believe that there are two gods, rivals as it were, the one the Artificer of good and the other of evil. There are also those who call the better one a god and the other a daemon, as, for example, Zoroaster the sage, who, they record, lived five thousand years before the time of the Trojan War. He called the one Oromazes and the other Areimanius; and he further declared that among all the things perceptible to the senses, Oromazes may best be compared to light, and Areimanius, conversely, to darkness and ignorance, and midway between the two is Mithras; for this reason the Persians give to Mithras the name of "Mediator." Zoroaster has also taught that men should make votive offerings and thank-offerings to Oromazes, and averting and mourning offerings to Areimanius. They pound up in a mortar a certain plant called *omomi* [= *haoma*], at the same time invoking Hades and Darkness; then they mix it with the blood of a wolf that has been sacrificed and carry it out and cast it into a place where the sun never shines. In fact, they believe that some of the plants belong to the good god and others to the evil daemon; so

also of the animals they think that dogs, fowls, and hedgehogs, for example, belong to the good god, but that water-rats belong to the evil one; therefore the man who has killed the most of these they hold to be fortunate.

It appears to be established that there were many individuals and groups who identified themselves as magi, or who were identified by others as such. These were by no means limited to the Iranian political sphere. Such individuals are recorded as having lived in Greece, Alexandria, Elephantine, and the western oases in Egypt, Asia Minor, the Caucuses, as well as in India and China.

MITHRAIC HISTORY

The history of the Magians is rather shrouded in mystery and complexity. Because the terms were used for a variety of institutions in the Iranian world and by people interacting with that world on its periphery, the precise movement of members of the class is hard to pinpoint. What is certain is that they were highly influential and that they acted as advisers and sources of learning and philosophy not only for their own culture but neighboring peoples as well. The story of the Mithraists is a bit more concrete, due to the many documents by classical authors referring to them and a remarkable array of archaeological evidence.

It is now well established that there was a martial cult of Mithra among the military in the Persian ceremonial capital of Persepolis about 500 BCE. When Mithraism was first being discussed among scholars in the West it was assumed that the cult had its origins in Persia. There were many obvious signs for this, but later and more recent scholars have tried to make the case for it being a purely Roman cult with just some dress-up features imitating Persian symbols with no real Persian content. One of the main tenets for this was that it was believed that there was no Persian cult of Mithra. This has been proved to be categorically false. There was a vibrant cult of Mithra in the Persian Empire *among soldiers*. It is most likely that this cult was not identical to that of Western Mithraism and that it was understood entirely within the framework of Zoroastrian orthodoxy. In Zoroastrianism, Mithra is seen as man's best friend in the pantheon and to be an intermediary between humans and the Amesha Spentas ("Bounteous Immortals").

The Persian Empire of the Achaemenids was conquered by the Macedonian king Alexander (the Great) in 331 BCE. This instituted a period of intense Hellenization in the territories of the former Persian Empire for about a century after Alexander's conquest. Over time the Iranians overthrew the political forms left by Alexander, and in any event the Macedonian king had always been anxious to Persianize his court as much as possible. He had all of his leading men marry Persian women, for example. Generally speaking, however, it must be understood that the time period between 312 and 248 BCE remains one that is often quite mysterious as to what sorts of exchanges took place. One thing is certain: massive amounts of cultural interchange were undertaken. It is in the realm of Hellenic-Iranian syncretism, or blending, that a synthesis of the Iranian sequence of iconic images suggested by the Zoroastrian calendar used by the Persian elites was Hellenized and brought into accord with the twenty-four-term system determined by the Greek letters (*stoicheia*) of their alphabet. This system is outlined in chapter 3 of this work.

THE RISE OF MITHRAISM IN THE WEST AMONG THE ROMANS

To understand how the ancient initiatory system of Mithraism might have shaped the original sequence of icons that ultimately resulted in the tarot, we must first outline what Mithraism is—its origins, tenets, and mythology.

Ultimately, Mithraism should be considered a distant branch of Iranian religion. Most early scholars saw this as being the likely fact, while later scholars drifted into insisting that Mithraism was a purely Roman phenomenon with burlesque Persian images. The truth is certainly somewhere in between. Although it is deeply rooted in the prehistoric traditions of the Indo-Europeans, our archaeological record for the

Roman practice of Mithraism as a fixed and independent mystery cult in the West shows that it was introduced over a time period spanning between about 66 BCE and 66 CE. However, the relationship between original Iranian cult of Mithra and the mystery cult of the Romans focused on Mithras (which appears to have influenced the tradition of the tarok) probably began in a formal manner but was fairly quickly transformed by the needs and experiences of the initiates of the Roman West. On the surface, the contents of the Roman cult of Mithras may seem more philosophically Roman than Iranian, and even more Greek than Iranian. But appearances can be—and often are—deceiving. The basic underlying impetus and symbolism of the faith remained rooted in the Iranian system. This is specifically demonstrated throughout the contents of this book.

The cult of Mithra was important among many Iranian people and was especially so among the Parthians, who, as we have seen, reconquered parts of northern Iran from the Hellenistic rulers left behind by Alexander. The cult practiced by the leaders of these people was centered on Mithra, an ancient (and pre-Zoroastrian) god of justice and kingship, and who also remained an important *yazata* in Zoroastrianism itself. We know that Mithra was worshipped throughout the Parthian Empire and that his cult was especially centered on the kings and their personal retinues of warriors. The magûs (sg. *magû*) were priests who participated in the cult and Mysteries of Mithra and are said by some to have employed a nocturnal bloody sacrifice of bulls and horses. These liturgical characteristics clearly distinguish this kind of Mithraism from the philosophically based moral dualism of orthodox Zoroastrianism. It is also likely that no actual animal sacrifice was carried out as a part of the Mysteries of Mithras in the West, except insofar as they were already part of the Roman cult of state, incorporated into Mithraic practice later on. It is certainly true, however, that the use of the symbol of fire was common to the liturgy of both Magianism and Zoroastrianism. This is chiefly because Zoroaster (Zarathustra), a priest trained in the national cults of the ancient Iranians, retained many of the external forms of the religion, while abstracting and reinterpreting their significances in a more rational and philosophical way based on his world-shattering insight (Av. *Daêna*) that there was no absolute god other than "pure focused consciousness." He called this entity by the name Ahura Mazda (Lord-Wisdom), and rationally intuited that all other gods and goddesses were actually emanations of this one divinity. It is also more than likely that the cult of Mithra practiced within the Persian army going all the way back to the Achaemenids was far more in keeping with Zoroastrian teachings than the later Parthian version, since the Parthians were originally a sort of seminomadic and culturally more archaic Iranian nation from the northwestern part of the empire.

The philosophical moral dualism of the orthodox Zoroastrians was based not on world-denying emotions but rather on rational, world-affirming principles: the good and wise god (Ahura Mazda, or Ohrmazd) created a perfect world, which was beset and corrupted by evil entities, where humanity exists as the comrade and coworker with this Ahura Mazda to restore the good creation. Those things are classified as *good* which promote the happiness, well-being, prosperity, strength, courage, intelligence, and wisdom within creation; those things are seen as *evil* (or bad) which promote misery, sickness, poverty, weakness, cowardice, stupidity, and ignorance.

It has been said that there is no sign of Ohrmazd in the lore of the Roman Mithraists. However, it appears that, in a henotheistic fashion, Mithra(s) absorbed many of the characteristics of the high god of the Iranians and was reconceptualized not as an adjunct god but as the high god himself.

As we have seen, the magûs were the priests of the western and northern Iranian cults, and they were not always entirely orthodox Zoroastrians. Some appear to have focused their philosophical system on Zurvan (Eternal Time or Destiny), while others focused on Mithra (the mediator between Ohrmazd, the God of Light, and Ahriman, the God of Darkness). The interest in time and its divisions as related to the determination of destiny seems to have been an influence from the Babylonian and Hellenic worlds upon the Iranians.

Mithraism and Magianism began to spread westward from home bases in the Parthian Empire about the time of the beginning of our era and became established by the middle of the first century CE. By then the cult of the Iranian priests had become well established in Mesopotamia, the Levant (present-day Israel and Lebanon), in the northern parts of present-day Turkey, and throughout the regions of present-day Armenia and Azerbaijan. There was a Magian contingent in Alexandria and a temple of Mithra has been found there.

The Roman historian Dio Cassius (155–235 CE) writes about the name Mithras being spoken of during the visit of the Armenian king Tiridates I to Rome at the time of Nero. Tiridates I was the son of Vonones II of Parthia, whose coronation by Nero in the year 66 CE sealed a peace treaty between Parthia and Rome. Some say it was this connection that brought in the Mithraic Mysteries.

The important thing to realize about this cult of the magûs is that when members of it migrated beyond the boundaries of the areas where their cult was dominant, they often became agents of syncretism, whereby elements of Iranian thought were expressed through foreign mythic imagery. They absorbed and synthesized elements from every religious and magical system with which they came into contact. Astrological lore was absorbed from the Babylonians, and the gods and goddesses of the Greeks, Romans, Phrygians, Thracians, and Egyptians all found correspondences with the Iranian pantheon of divinities and abstract principles.

During the first century CE, as the Roman legions continued to be in conflict, and thus close contact, with the Parthians, the Mithraic Mysteries began to spread rapidly throughout the Roman Empire. It was carried by Roman legions who had become initiated into the warrior-mysteries of Mithras (as his name was Hellenized). By the third or fourth century CE, Mithraism had spread throughout the entire Roman Empire—from Britain to Alexandria, and from the Rhineland to Rome itself. To judge from the distribution of Mithraea (Mithraic temples), the cult was especially popular in the northern reaches of the empire, along the Rhine and Danube, and on the Italian peninsula itself.

During its spread, Mithraism adopted many of the outer theological forms of the classical host cultures—the old gods and goddesses of the Iranians merely changed their names and external forms to be more socially, politically, and psychologically acceptable to insiders and outsiders alike.

The spread and success of the Iranian cult of Mithra in the West is a remarkable phenomenon simply because it is an element taken from a culture with which both the Greeks and the Romans carried on one of the most prolonged and apparently bitter cultural, economic, and military conflicts in the history of the world. This battle between East and West may lie at the very roots of our present-day paradigm of geo-political struggle. But just as it is often thought that many crusading knights fell in with Sufis in the Holy Land, the Greeks and Romans may have similarly interacted with the predecessors of the Sufis—the ancient Iranian practical philosophers.

But to gain a fuller understanding of what Roman Mithraism is, it is perhaps necessary to mention some of the things that it most certainly is *not*.

Mithraism is not orthodox Zoroastrianism. It is a common error to assume that Mithraism is virtually the same as Zoroastrianism. Both draw on the same underlying mythic material, just as Judaism, Christianity, and Islam draw on a common mythic background (the Judaic), but they all constitute distinct, even if interrelated, systems. In fact, there is probably more *essential* difference between Mithraism and Zoroastrianism than there is between Judaism and Islam. However, because the whole of the world was greatly influenced by Iranian ideas, its philosophy, mythology, and symbolism permeated much more than people are generally aware of today.

Zoroastrianism exemplifies a moralistic dualism. The distinction between good and evil exists primarily on a *moral* plane. There are prohibitions against animal sacrifice, nocturnal worship, and the whole ultra-violent warrior ethic of the most ancient Iranian kings and chieftains. Zarathustra himself may have been assassinated by a band of warriors because of his attempts to overthrow the traditional social organization. It is of the utmost importance to understand that there is no strict dichotomy between the "spiritual creation" (*menog*) and the "material creation" (*getik*). In fact, according to Zoroastrian doctrine, the material creation is sometimes considered *more* holy than the merely spiritual because it completes and objectifies what had only existed *in potentia* before.

In orthodox Zoroastrian terms, the Mithraism could be considered a form of *daêva* worship. The daêvas are some of the old pre-Zoroastrian god-forms of the Iranians, which the orthodox Zoroastrians identify as demons. However, the external liturgical forms of worship of the ancient Iranians were largely retained by the Zoroastrians—this they continued to hold in common with other Iranian sects. The meanings of the external forms and symbols might be different, but those are often impossible to distinguish, given the external similarities. This being said, the figure and deity known as Mithra was fully incorporated into the mythic theology of the Zoroastrians as a yazata—"one worthy of worship"—and retained his place of high honor within the religion.

Mithraism is not Manicheanism. Mani (215–276 CE), the prophet who gave expression to a new religion, created a particular Zoroastrian heresy, which stated that the "Good Creation" is the equivalent of the *spiritual* world, and the "Evil Creation" is the equivalent of the *material* world. This is totally at odds with the meanings of both orthodox Zoroastrianism (in which the physical world is seen in principle as a perfect reflection of the divine pattern) and with Zurvanite Mithraism (in which the physical world is cheerfully accepted as a mixture of good and evil). Manicheanism was adapted to Judeo-Christian mythology, where it gave rise to many heretical sects in the Middle Ages (Bogomils, Cathars, Waldensians, etc.). It is also clear that the ideas of Zarathustra were adopted, albeit poorly and inaccurately, by Judeo-Christian sects known as the Gnostics beginning in the early decades of the Common Era. The dualism expressed by these sects was inspired by Zarathustra, although the essence of what the Gnostics taught was most usually at odds with the life- and world-affirming message of Zarathustra and his orthodox followers.

It is most likely that the Mithrists were no more morally dualistic than the ancient Germanic and Slavic tribes with whom they share many mythological patterns. The Mithraic solution to the inherently dualistic structure of Iranian myth was essentially Zurvanite. Zurvan is the ancient Iranian god of Eternal Time, who would be identified as the Greek Aiôn. Apparently an extremely archaic Iranian conception and one that would not be eliminated by Zoroastrian philosophical orthodoxy, Eternal Time (or Destiny) as an androgynous being gave birth to two sons: Ohrmazd and Ahriman, who sprang from his shoulders. This eldest of the gods, Zurvan, is then made the creator of both good and evil, which implies an ambiguous mixture of these two qualities, in the cosmos from the beginning. This appears to be the attitude of the Mithrist. Ancient Mithrists did not diabolize Ahriman or the daêvas—indeed every known fact about Mithraic practice points to it being classified as a sort of daêva-worship from an orthodox Zoroastrian viewpoint. Such worship was most usually tolerated within the Persian Empire itself in the most ancient times, as it was merely seen as a holdover from pre-Zoroastrian Iranian religion. But Roman Mithraism was more than that, as it became a mechanism for the synthesizing of ideas from a wide variety of cultural and mythic spheres.

As a mystery cult, Mithraism was also unique in that it was not dependent upon a single sanctuary or location to which *mystae* (sg. *mystēs*) were attracted to be initiated, but rather it was a system of thousands of thriving Mithraic initiatory locations, the Mithraea scattered over the whole continent of Europe. This is not a matter of speculation or interpretation, as the archaeological remains of these sites are still there for us to see today. As we delve deeper into the history and meaning of Mithraism, we may come to understand that the myths, aims, and purposes of the Roman cult were in fact far more in harmony with those of the orthodox Zoroastrians than some had previously thought.

In the final analysis it will be discovered that the aims of orthodox Zoroastrianism and those of Mithraism—the transformation of individuals, society, and the cosmos itself into a better and more ideal form—can lead us to the conclusion that the cult of Mithras was perhaps a skillful insinuation of the ideas of Zarathustra into the Western world by means of a classic tactic of the Mazmaga, the Great Fellowship. The only sad thing is that the experiment ultimately failed, as the Mysteries of Mithras were wiped out. But they have survived underground and are being revived today as well.

MITHRAIC COSMOLOGY

What we know about Mithraic doctrines must be gleaned from analysis of their archaeological remnants (in the art of the Mithraea), from what pagan Greek and Roman writers said about them, from what their enemies in the early Christian church wrote about them, and from comparative evidence drawn from Iranian texts that, while they are not purely Mithraic, often give otherwise unavailable insight into the roots of Mithraic thought. No original Mithraic texts have survived. This is doubtlessly due to systematic persecution by the Christian church, coupled with the fact that the priests and initiates of the Mysteries of Mithras, being a secret cult, probably did not write down much of their occult teachings.

The Iranian cosmological myths are closely related to the other Indo-European myths concerning the origin of the order of the world from India to Scandinavia. There are two beings from which the present order of the world came into being: a cosmic man (called Gâyomart in the Iranian tradition) and a cosmic ox. From the seed of the primeval man come the original human beings and from his body are produced the "seven metals" (= the planets/gods); and from the marrow of the ox come all manner of beneficial plants, and from his seed come all species of animals.

In ancient Iranian myth it is conspicuously related how Ahriman, in league with his female consort Jeh, slew the ox or bull or caused its death through disease. Some have seen that in Mithraism, Ahriman was somehow replaced in this cosmogonic process by Mithras. This would seem to be incorrect. Clearly from the image of the tauroctony, the bull sacrifice of Mithras is seen as an act that is *beneficial* to both the world and to the individual. Also, the image represents a mythic or symbolic reality rather than actual ritual. Within Zoroastrian myth this image is perhaps best clarified by the idea presented in the end-of-times myth contained in the *Bundahishn* (XXX, 25). It tells of how the final Saoshyant, or world savior, performs the last sacrifice of the bull Hadhayos. From the fat of the bull, mixed with the white Haoma, "they prepare Hush and give it to all men, and thus all men become immortal. . . ." This ancient Iranian myth of the end of times is liturgically transferred to any shift in ages and to any end of great cycles. This connects the idea to the ideal of the perfection of individual human beings as well.

Ancient Iranian myth shared a constellation of entities at the beginning of time with the Indian and Germanic mythic worlds. These entities are, among others, a cosmic man and a cosmic bovine. The world is brought into being and order established as the result of a sacrifice. Things are begun and ended in similar ways in ritual practice. The tauroctony is a symbol of renewal—of the individual, of society, and of the cosmos. Mithra became a figure associated with this process—so much so that his name is attached to the apocalyptic mythic figure of Maitreya (< Skt. *Mitra* = Av. *Mithra*) in some Buddhist teachings.

The myth of Mithras's bull slaying has been reconstructed by Cumont as follows:[1]

One day Mithras attempted to capture the cosmic bull, which was grazing in the mountains. The divine hero jumped on the bull's back and seized him by the horns. Although the bull was able to throw Mithras off, the hero never let go of the horns. He was thus dragged along the ground, where he suffered terribly—but he never released the horns. Eventually, the bull was exhausted and Mithras dragged him by the hind feet to his home, which was in a cave. (The dragging of Mithras was called the *transitus,* and is a symbol of man's sufferings.)

The bull, however, succeeded in escaping from the cave and again roamed in the mountains. The divinity of the Sun sent his messenger, the raven, to Mithras to tell him to slay the bull. Mithras did not want to do this deed, but was commanded to do so by the Solar deity, and so he obeyed. He set out to hunt the beast with his trusty dog. They hunted the cosmic bull back to the cave where Mithras was able to deliver a deadly blow to the back of the animal with his knife. This is the scene of the *tauroktonia* (bull-slaying) which is displayed in the apse of virtually every Mithraeum. It is quite possible that the original name of the "tarot" (*tarok*) derives from this word *taurok-tonia*.

From the spinal column of the bull sprang wheat (the source of man's daily bread and that which is sacrificed in the Mysteries), from his blood sprang the vine (the source of the sacred drink of the Mysteries), and from his seed (which was purified by the Moon; see *Bundahishn,* ch. X) sprang all beneficial animals. Thus, Mithras facilitated the creation of the world as we know it.

Another important cosmological function of Mithras involves his chariot, or *quadriga,* pulled by four cosmic horses. They circumambulate the pole in the north. The outermost horse is fiery and moves with great velocity around the pole; the next (airy) one moves slower and the next (watery) one slower still; and finally, the innermost (earthy) horse stands in one place and turns at the pole. The fire of the breath of the first horse ignites the mane of the innermost horse and the four are transformed into a single quintessential whole.[2]

It is clear that due to certain early Babylonian influences Mithraic cosmology was significantly reformed along astrological lines. The number seven and the lore of the planets (and seven metals) became an important part of every phase of Mithraic teachings. This does not seem to have been a part of the original purely Iranian system, but it quickly became an integral part of Mithraic lore and teachings. However, it is possible that the Mithrists were not interested in astrology on a practical level but rather saw the planets (gods) as symbols for certain states of being. This speculation is fueled by the fact that the seven Mithraic grades of initiation have planetary correspondences that do not match the natural order: the peculiar Mithraic sequence is Mercury, Venus, Mars, Jupiter, Luna, Sol, and Saturn.

Cumont dismisses Mithraic astrological speculations as "nothing more than intellectual diversions designed to amuse the neophytes."[3] More recent work by David Ulansey seems to show that these speculations were much more than mere "intellectual diversions," but at the same time we must keep in mind that it was the significance behind the astrological phenomena—and not the mere physical events themselves—that Mithraic ideology and initiation encoded.

Stoicism is the philosophical school in the Hellenistic world that seems to have most influenced the teachings of Mithraism. This is perhaps so because the roots of Stoicism probably go back to even more ancient Iranian ideas, which began to be imported into the West in the middle of the sixth century in Greece. Stoicism came to the fore in third-century Greece and stems from the ideas of Heraclitus (535–475 BCE), who was a native of the city of Ephesus, which was part of the Persian Empire during his lifetime. These ideas became the quasi-official philosophy of the late Roman Republic and early Imperial period. As a moral philosophy, it stresses personal duty and discipline, two virtues highly prized by Mithraist soldiers. Stoicism also held teachings on the soul and its immortality, as well as regarding the abstract reality of the gods. In the main, however, the Stoic believed in the implacable hand of Destiny, of the power of Fortuna and Iustitia. For the Stoic, Fortuna was not arbitrary, she is governed by the movements of the stars—which is another way of saying the mechanical universe. The Stoic knows his earthly life is subject to Fortuna, but he also realizes that his soul can be trained to free itself from these constraints. But because such training can only be achieved in this mundane life, the trials and tribulations of life are cheerfully accepted.

One of the centers of Stoic philosophy happened to be Tarsus in Cilicia (in present-day Turkey), where Plutarch had reported that the pirates of that region were worshippers of Mithras. It seems to have been from this epicenter that western Mithraism quickly spread throughout the Roman Empire.

Perhaps one of the innovations absorbed into the cult in Tarsus was the discovery by Stoic astronomers of the phenomenon of the precession of the equinoxes. This astronomical phenomenon results from the fact that the Earth wobbles slightly on its axis, causing the celestial equator to move through the zodiacal band of stars over time. Thus the phenomenon of the equinox actually makes a precession through the zodiacal signs—moving through one sign every 2,160 years. This astronomical phenomenon can be seen from two perspectives—that of the apparent movement of the polar axis of the Earth and that of the apparent movement of the point in the zodiacal signs in which the equinox takes place.

Stoic philosopher-scientists thought of the stars and their movements as a map of the implacable force of Destiny (Gk. εἰμαρμένη). With the discovery of the phenomenon of the precession of the equinoxes, a force that even caused the stars to bend to its will was discovered. This previously hidden divinity then became the focus of a secret mystery cult—which insinuated itself into the Mithraism that was emerging in Tarsus at approximately the same time the discovery was made.

One of the great attractions the cult of Mithraism held out in the ancient world was the fact that it was able to incorporate all of the known scientific data of the time into a religious and initiatory system.

As far as its genesis is concerned, however, everything points to the Mithrists originating not among dualistic sects of Iranian religion but rather among the many still daêva-worshipping national cults of the Iranian people. This does not mean, however, that they had no notion of good and evil or that they did not see themselves as warriors fighting for the good and against the evil but merely that they did not accept the orthodox Zoroastrian definitions of these categories.

MITHRAIC INITIATION

Mithraism was a mystery cult, which means that the progressive revelation of mysteries to the mystēs, or initiate, was central to its teachings and methods. Despite whatever the immediate origins of Roman Mithraism might have been, the ultimate origin of the Mithraic Mysteries clearly lies in the extremely archaic warrior societies of the Indo-Iranians. The roots of the Mithraic system of initiation go back to the archaic traditions of the Persian and Parthian tribes of Iranian warriors and developed over several centuries, absorbing traits from various cultures and philosophical systems, until the cult of Mithraism was finally extinguished in the last years of the Roman Empire.

The fact that the Mysteries had their roots in warrior societies in the East, and that even in their final stages of development in the Roman West remained largely limited to males (many of whom were indeed soldiers), is significant. This shows the continuity of the essence of the Mysteries, regardless of whatever scientific or auxiliary teachings might have been attached to them over time.

One of the essential secrets of the archaic warrior societies was the secret of personal transformation. As the warrior passed through the various grades or degrees of initiation into the warrior society, he was progressively transformed into a more perfect warrior and being. One of the essential components of this was the teaching of the skill of shapeshifting. Chief among these in ancient times was the ability of young warriors to shift their "shapes" into those of wolves. This was because wolves were admired for their cunning power as hunters and for their social structure. It is this type of tradition that is ultimately responsible for the zoomorphic symbolism in the Mithraic initiatory system.

That which is actually initiated—or transformed—in the Mysteries is the soul. Before human bodies were created, souls were shaped and existed. Some of these entered into incarnation because of the compulsion of Necessity—by natural force. According to the tradition of Zarathustra, the vast majority of humans have come into their bodies by their own wills, and they have volunteered to enter into the cosmic battle against the infection of the world by evil forces led by Angra Mainyu (or Ahriman). These are the warrior-souls and can be technically identified with the *fravashis* (a person's individual soul). They (we) carry out the battle against the forces of ignorance, cruelty, and poverty in the world.

Initiation is a process of the ascent of the soul back through the planetary spheres through which it came into incarnation from the realm beyond the stars. In a natural context, this is a postmortem phenomenon—through initiation, however, one can experience this process while still living.

The ordering of the planetary spheres seems peculiar to the Mithraic Mysteries. This is not because Mithraists were ignorant of the scientific cosmology of the day but because, initiatorily, the candidate cycled through the spheres in a magically determined way, as shown in the figure below.

This rhythm, or frequency pattern of motion, through the planetary spheres also has a bearing on the ordering of the tarok images. It explains, for example, why the celestial triad of Stars-Moon-Sun (with the Comet or Devil apparently acting as a catalyst) is essential.

As the candidate passes through each grade/planetary sphere, certain qualities are stripped away and others received or perfected—each according to the nature and character of the planetary sphere in question.

Cycling beyond the Moon to Mercury, base desires would be abandoned to that divinity and noble desires perfected; and cycling to Venus, harmful appetites would be purified into an appetite for truth. Cycling beyond the Sun to Mars, the initiate would abandon anger and irrational violence and don a mantle of courage; and cycling to Jupiter, all illusory dreams would be given up for a sublime determination and will. The candidate would then cycle toward the Stars—but

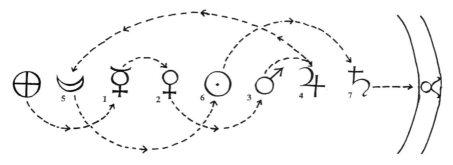

The Mithraic Initiatory Cycle

would, if the initiatory journey was to continue, be drawn back to the realm of the Moon, where his old vital and nutritive energies would be relinquished to be replaced by immortal ones. From the Moon he would cycle toward the Sun, where false doctrines and ideas are rejected for a pure and direct intellective faculty. Finally, the candidate passes through the gate of Saturnus, who is the Father and who guards the passage into the realm of the Stars of the Zodiac. This initiatory passage is keyed to the initiatory grades of the Mithraic Mysteries as discussed below.

But parallel to this gradual and rational development of the soul to an immortalized and enlightened state, there is a doctrine of a sudden and miraculous transformation of the body into an immortal and eternally happy condition. As opposed to the spiritual path of initiation, this transfiguration of the body can take place only at the end of the cycle of time. At that moment a savior, a Saoshyant, will appear as an incarnation of Mithras and a cosmic bull will also appear. The Saoshyant will call forth the bodies of the dead back to life—and all will recognize one another because they will have the physical appearances they had in their earlier lives. This is the promised Final Body. Then the new Mithras will sacrifice the divine bull and mingle its fat with the consecrated drink known as Haoma. This drink of immortality will be given to the wise and just so that they will become perfect and immortal (in perfect and beautiful physical bodies so that they can enjoy the fullness of life). Some say this drink will be denied to those who remained ignorant and wicked. Those who have been judged as lacking will be punished. Most will be able to be purified enough to enjoy the drink of immortality, while some say that others will be annihilated utterly. Some, guided by logic, say that the all-wise and all-good Creator, for whom the souls of humans volunteered to enter into the earthbound battleground, would never utterly and eternally condemn members of this volunteer army just because they were so wounded and traumatized by the battle that they made many wrong choices.

As mentioned earlier, there are seven grades of Mithraic initiation. Those belonging to the three outer grades are called "servitors," and those belonging to the inner grades are called "participants." The grades each had a Latin title and planetary significance as outlined below.

Servitors:	1. Corax = Crow or Raven	= Mercury
	2. Cryphius = Occult (or Nymphus = Groom)	= Venus
	3. Miles = Soldier	= Mars
Participants:	4. Leo = Lion	= Jupiter
	5. Mithra = Mithras (or Perses = Persian)	= Luna
	6. Heliodromus = Courier of the Sun	= Sol
	7. Pater = Father	= Saturn

The second and fifth grades had two variant titles. Cryphius indicated one who was taken into the secret confines of the cult—who had in some sense married, becoming a groom to some secret bride within the cult. Originally, this probably had some sexual mystery attached to it. Perses (the Persian) was simply a euphemism for the more explicit Mithras, who was, to the Romans, the Persian god.

Even young boys could be admitted to the first three grades. The animal designations for some of the grades are probably vestiges of the oldest stage of these rites among the ancient Iranian warbands sometimes referred to in the scholarly literature as "men's societies" (Ger. *Männerbünde*). These made up the cultic side of the warrior societies in the most archaic Indo-European times—and they served as the continuing basis for non-Zoroastrian Iranian religions.

What we know of the initiatory significance of these grades is limited to what we can glean from the artwork found in the Mithraea themselves, and from certain (usually hostile) written descriptions by outsiders.

We know that the mystēs was required to take a *sacramentum,* or oath, to keep the secrets of the Mysteries. There was a lustration, or baptism-like rite, for entry into the grade of Soldier. The candidate was offered a crown, which he refused, declaring Mithras to be his only crown. He would then be branded on the forehead with a hot iron. This practice may have been borrowed from a method used by Roman soldiers to seal their oaths of loyalty. It is also possibly a reference to the Iranian tradition of a stream of molten metal by which the soul will be punished/purified in the postmortem realm.

Upon entry into the participant grade of the Lion, the ritual use of water for ablutions was renounced, and thus entry was marked by having the candidate's hands and tongue coated with honey—which is said to have come from the Moon. This is a sign of the triumph of Fire over Water. Honey is a preservative agent, which makes one wise and the cohort of the gods themselves. At this level the initiate received the sacrament of bread and water, which was mixed with bull's urine. (Even today Zoroastrian initiatory rites are marked by the drinking of a bit of bull's urine, which is said to have the power of purification.)

Other aspects of their rites included a simulated murder, fighting a symbolic monstrous enemy, and climbing a ladder made of seven rungs of seven metals—lead, tin, bronze, iron, alloy (of gold and silver), silver, and gold.

The Mithraic Mysteries were never said to have been orgiastic, but there were many severe physical ordeals, including flagellation, being bound and blindfolded, and the aforementioned branding on the forehead. One painting in a Mithraeum shows a candidate blindfolded and bound naked, with a priest standing before him offering him a sword.

One of the most important rituals of the Mithraic liturgy was a sacramental meal offered to the Pater of the conventicle. This was to commemorate the meal shared between Mithras and Sol after the slaying of the cosmic bull.

The essential function of the Mithraic cult was the initiation of its members. This initiation had less in common with the Greek and Egyptian Mysteries and more in common with the extremely archaic initiatory rites of Indo-Iranian men's societies. Magical technology was applied to the development of the individual—the individual was educated, magically transformed, and ultimately experienced a salvation that conferred immortality. Roman Mithraism combined these powerful archaic elements with a state-of-the-art understanding of the Stoic science current in the empire to create a synthesis that was exotic and mysterious while at the same time being seen as scientific and accurate. The Mithraist participated in ancient rites and learned eldritch lore— which satisfied his soul—and learned of astronomical and scientific truths, which he thought perfected his mind and intellect. With this understanding provided by the Mysteries, the Mithraist could control Destiny—the ultimate initiatory achievement of the Magian.

THE DIVINITIES OF MITHRAISM

Mithraism inherited divinities from the ancient Iranian pantheon, but these were usually understood to be the equivalents of the gods and goddesses of other peoples with whom the Magians came into contact. Many Iranians, at least for a time after the age of Alexander the Great, were almost as enthusiastic about syncretizing foreign gods as the Greeks were. This process had begun in Mesopotamia, where the Iranian pantheon had been syncretized with the astral divinities of Semitic Babylon, and it continued as the Magians encountered the gods and goddesses of the Greeks, Romans, and even Egyptians.

Orthodox Zoroastrianism rejected the ancient Iranian plurality of gods and goddess in favor of a more monotheistic view that saw Ohrmazd (Ahura Mazda) as the One True God and other divinities as either angelic beings surrounding this divinity and helping it to transform the world (the *amesha spentas* or *yazatas*), or as demonic beings opposing this plan (the *daêvas*). The name Ahura Mazda is a combination of a masculine and a feminine principle: Lord-Wisdom. It is philosophically beyond gender. But in the case of the Mithrists (and many Magians) there was a tendency to hold on to the old gods and goddesses in their fully polytheistic meaning without the larger philosophical understanding encoded in orthodox Zoroastrianism.

THE GODS

If we assume that the most popular theology of the western part of the Parthian Empire at the time of the rise of Roman Mithraism was the

Zurvanite version of Zoroastrianism and that this also was the prevailing philosophy of the Magians of the time, then we must deal with the essence of Zurvanite thinking. Zurvanism seems to have gained considerable influence as a philosophical construct during the Sasanian period (224–651 CE) and is really best known from foreign sources, not from internal Zoroastrian texts. It was probably a formalization of a general older tendency.

Perhaps the best way of understanding the roots of this concept philosophically is to compare the idea to what we find in Germanic mythology. This comparison is not drawn out of the blue; rather it is known that the Iranian tribes such as the Scythians and Sarmatians had a heavy influence on the Germanic peoples at the time when the latter were coming into being as a distinct group, circa 700 to 600 BCE. Thus some of the most characteristic Germanic cosmological conceptions seem to have been drawn from these Iranian sources. The *Edda* tells us of the evolution of the gods (*æsir*) and giants (*þurses*) out of an androgynous entity (Ymir) in a dim and timeless pre-aionic age. There were also entities called the Norns, which are distinctly models of time: their names are Urðr, Verðandi, and Skuld ("That which has become," "That which is becoming," and "That which should happen"). These cosmic forces subject even the gods to their power. They are, however, largely impersonal and almost abstract. So here we can clearly see that the gods and their eternal foes, the þurses, spring from a common source and are in continual battle with one another. It seems that this type of conception is similar to what proto-Zurvanism must have been like.

Zurvanism in all likelihood represented a syncretism between and among various Near Eastern ways of thinking that were part of the Hellenistic world. The dominant elements in this syncretic mix were Greek, Roman (Stoic), Hebrew, Chaldaic (Aramaic), Egyptian, Gnostic (Christian), and, of course, Persian. Because the Mithrists were drawn from all sorts of people, the level of syncretism—of blending together elements from different streams into one new system—must have been very high.

The major reason why Zurvanism cannot be seen as the original form of the religion founded by the prophet Zarathustra is because it limits the absolute goodness and wisdom of Ahura Mazda (Ohrmazd), and the reason why it was eventually overcome within Zoroastrianism is because it limits the power of the individual choice of unique human beings. An important feature of Zurvanism is the idea of the over-whelming power of destiny, fate, the power of the mechanism of the planetary bodies, and so forth.

The major gods of Magianism are Zurvan (Eternal Time) and his two sons Ohrmazd and Ahriman (the first, the Son of Light and Goodness; the second, the Son of Darkness and Evil), with Mithra as an intermediary between them. Mithra could be identified with either Ohrmazd or Ahriman on occasion. The fact that he became the focus of the royal cult of the Pahlavis (Parthians) demonstrates the continued ability of that Iranian nation to balance the Darkness and the Light. They did so by focusing on the Eternal Transcendent (Zurvan) and the Victorious Savior (Mithra).

Zurvan

In the iconography of the Mithraea there is an unnamed divinity that has been identified as the Greek Aiôn and naturally connected to the Iranian concept of Zurvan, "Time." Zurvan (or Zurvân) is not a divinity in orthodox Zoroastrianism but instead is a feature of indigenous Iranian belief. In later times Zurvan became a coagulation of every imaginable divine force. Cumont says that he is "ineffable, bereft alike of name, sex, and passions."[4] As the illustration on page 58 shows, the iconography of the god demonstrates attributes of all of the major "Olympians." There are six coils of the serpent's body around that of the god; these are the six lower planets, with the Sun on the leonine head. The four wings are emblematic of the four seasons and lower elements. The two keys refer to Zurvan's role as the "monarch of heaven whose portals he opens." He holds a scepter, which refers to his divine sovereignty. The thunderbolt equates him with Jupiter, and the caduceus with Mercury. The hammer and tongs point to his equation with Vulcan—who is the *interpretatio Romana* of the Iranian Atar, the Sacred Fire. The cock and pinecone refer to Asclepius. The Stoicizing Mithraists equated Zurvan with the Supreme Cause. He is known as the progenitor of all the gods and so was at one time or another equated with the Greek Aion (Roman Saeculum) and Kronos (Roman Saturnus) and thus linked with the concept of Destiny or Fatality (Gk. εἱμαρμένη) and the original Divine Fire.

Zurvan cannot be worshipped or appealed to in prayer. There is really no record of a cult of Zurvan as such, but the concept plays an important role in the cosmology of the early Iranians and in the philosophy of the Sasanian court. This is a name of the Absolute. Mithra holds the key to the ascent of consciousness to the Zurvanite level. In Zoroastrianism, Ohrmazd is specifically referred to as a friend of mankind, whereas in Zurvanism, the high god is seen as a distant and implacable force. The role of friend of mankind is taken up by none other than Mithra. In many respects, the way in which Mithra becomes a link to the higher godhead is similar to the way in which Christians see Christ as a bridge to Jehovah—or the equivalent of Jehovah in the dominant sect.

The Avestan word *zurvân* means simply "time." The twenty-first sirozah mentions two types of time: infinite and the long autonomous. Infinite time is static and unchanging; the long autonomous time passes and can be measured. Most scholars agree that there was not really a cult of Zurvan separate from that of Ahura Mazda in Zoroastrian circles; it was just a philosophical stance toward the myths and events.

Mithra

Mithra is the theological focus of Mithrism, not Ohrmazd, who is the focus of the more orthodox sects of Iranian religion. It seems as though the most ancient Mithrists were among those who remained apart from the dualistic philosophical reforms of Zoroaster and who continued to worship in the older ways.

For Roman Mithraism, the god Mithras henotheistically assumed the role of the high god and was approached as the great power and godhead within the cult or Mysteries. The idea of "monotheism"—that is, the idea that there was one divine source of being and creation—was already well established in philosophical circles in Greece and Rome:

it was typically called the One, the Good, or the Light. Philosophical monotheism, tempered with the continued worship and honoring of historical gods and goddesses (seen as aspects of the One), is an attitude learned from the Persians.

In the original Iranian pantheon, Mithra is the god of legal matters, of contracts, and of law and order. The name "Mithra" actually translates to the word "contract." His function answers closely to that of Zeus in the Greek pantheon, Jupiter in the Roman, the Dagda (= "good god") in the Irish, and Týr in the Norse. In a way, Mithra made theological peace between the conservative and the reform-minded Iranians of the Alexandrian period, and under his banner perhaps a new synthesis was created.

According to Cumont, the central doctrine of Mithraism in the classical world involved the idea that Mithras is Light born out of solid rock.[5] That is, Mithras is the Light of the Stars radiating out of the Darkness of the sky (which the ancient Iranians thought of as being made of solid rock-crystal).

When Mithras manifested himself on Earth, he was also "born of rock" in a cave in the mountains. Only shepherds witnessed this event, which was marked by his torch (a shining star) above. The shepherds offered the infant gifts of their first fruits and flocks.[*]

After his birth, Mithras began to test his strength heroically against everything he met. Most important of these adventures is his slaying of the cosmic bull, the first creature of Ohrmazd. (This is recounted in some detail in the section on cosmology on page 27.) Mithras also overcame the power of the Sun and then formed a great alliance with him. The two became closely associated in Mithraic lore, and in some instances Mithras is identified with the solar power.

In the language of the times, Mithras is the Logos created by Jupiter-Ohrmazd so as to be able to create the natural order. Mithras

---

[*]If this sounds a bit like the Nativity of Jesus, it is no wonder—the myth of the birth of a savior was borrowed by many Jews, including the early Christians, from Iranian lore, which was popular and extremely prestigious in the Middle East at the time. The fact that the young Jesus is said to have been visited by three magi (wise men) from Persia (i.e., the East) is a remarkable testimony to this influence.

then also becomes the mediator between Heaven and Hell. His Greek title *mesitēs* ("mediator") refers to this, as does his medial position in the month: the sixteenth day.

"The Triple Mithras" refers to the images of Mithras flanked by the two torchbearers Cautes and Cautopates, who represent the rising and falling, waxing and waning powers of the sidereal manifestations of the god: the Stars, the Sun, and the Moon. Cautes is represented with a raised torch. He is also called Lucifer in Latin. He represents the beginning of the New Year at the spring equinox. On the other hand, Cautopates is also identified with the name Hesperus. He has a downward-turning torch and represents the fall equinox.

In the eventual Mithraic synthesis, Mithras became identified with the one true god with whom human religionists could hope to have any contact. Zurvan (Aion/Saturnus) was beyond any direct human contact and appeared unconcerned with human affairs.

Ohrmazd

Ohrmazd, Ahura Mazda of the Avestan times, is the morally good god of the Zoroastrians, but in Mithraism itself this god was a distant—if benevolent—unnamed or even unknown, grandfather figure. The original form of the name is often translated as "the Wise Lord." Mithras was the clear and present manifestation of the divine in the world and in human affairs. Although Ohrmazd is the ultimate cosmo-creator god, Mithras has more to do with the creation and maintenance of life on Earth. Mithras is the active agent of Ohrmazd in the material universe and a mediating force between the divine and mankind. It appears that, for Mithrists, the god Mithras assumed most of the functions of Ohrmazd.

Ahriman

Ohrmazd's brother or twin brother was called Ahriman. Different versions of the myth tell different stories: Ahriman emerged either shortly before or after Ohrmazd, and from either the shoulders or womb of their androgynous father/mother, Zurvan. Ahriman, whose Pahlavi name is derived from the older Avestan Angra Mainyu, "wicked spirit," attempted to overtake the realm of his brother and did this by attempting to create a material universe filled with destructive, vile, and parasitic entities. Ohrmazd, in defense of his moral standards, created a perfect material world, which acted as a bulwark against the acts of Ahriman. Thus thwarted, the evil one then proceeded to penetrate and pollute the good creation. Ahriman engineered a noxious counter-creation to oppose the will of Ohrmazd—and so the battle for the cosmos began.

The relationship between Mithras and the two divine brothers is highly ambiguous in the latter-day initiatory system of Mithraism itself. Perhaps this is because Mithras had exerted his mediating influence in the cult and he (and those who followed him) had begun the process of syncretizing the polar opposites in divinity generally thought to be represented by Ohrmazd and Ahriman.

Ahriman is philosophically understood to be the devil among the orthodox Zoroastrians. This was also a fate shared by some of the other old gods, or daêvas, of Iran. Mithra is among those notable for not having been so diabolized. But in ancient times the majority of Iranian sects was not dualistic in the philosophical Zoroastrian manner and continued to worship the various gods and goddesses of their ancestors in some way or another. Among them Ahriman was certainly problematic but not necessarily entirely evil.

In some Mithraic sites we find statues of a lion-headed god with the Latin dedicatory inscription **Deo Arimanio,** interpreted by many to mean: "To the god Ahriman." The fact that Mithras was perhaps sometimes identified among Mithraists themselves as the same god as Ahriman—in his role as the bull slayer—may clearly demonstrate the non-dualism of the Mithraists.

Another interpretation of this inscription and the Latin name of this god appears to be more accurate and telling: *Arimanius* does not refer to the Pahlavi name Ahriman at all but rather to another figure known in Manichean Middle Persian as Aryaman, in Pahlavi as Êrmân, whose name means "friend" and "member of the community." The Avestan noun *airyaman* corresponds to the Vedic *aryaman* and means "friend, companion." This is an archaic divinity in the Indo-Iranian pantheon. It is the same word that gives us "Aryan," meaning someone or something that is part of the community. The name and function seem to fit much better with the meaning of Mithras than they do with Ahriman!

In the Hellenistic age after the conquest of Persia by Alexander (331 BCE)—that is, during the time of the Seleucid Empire—the entirety of the Iranian pantheon, including the array of abstract principles that it enthroned, were given Greek and eventually Roman names. In doing this, the originally abstract, non-anthropomorphic entities of Iranian thought were apparently increasingly personified. But in fact, the reverse was equally true. In the philosophical atmosphere of late antique times in Greek and Roman culture, the old gods were easy to understand by philosophers as impersonal abstract principles that earlier had been subjected to personification by simple minds.

The comparative table below shows the common relationships among the divinities of various pantheons.

Iranian	Greek	Roman	Other
Zurvan	Aion/Kronos	Eon/Saturn	Abrasax (Hermetic)
Ohrmazd	Zeus	Jupiter	
Mithra(s)	Perseus		
Ahriman	Hades	Pluto	
Haoma	Dionysus	Bacchus	
Atar	Hephaestus	Vulcan	
Artagnes	Herakles	Hercules	
Shahrivar	Ares	Mars	
Apam-Nepat	Poseidon	Neptune	
Drvaspa		Silvanus	

THE GODDESSES

Much is often made of the fact that only men were admitted to the Mysteries of Mithras. This does not mean that women, or the divine in feminine form, were not important to the religion. It only means that the particular isolated form of the faith, which we see specifically represented in the Mithraea, is a largely all-male institution. There is evidence to show that this institution was less segregated with regard to gender in the early, pre-Roman period. It became increasingly sexually segregated as it moved westward and developed into an even more martial affair.

Anahita

The most important goddess in ancient Mithraism was Anahita, a name that was Hellenized to Anaitis. She is the consort of Mithra and originally the fourth Amesha Spenta, the goddess of Earth. She was thought to have three major manifestations, with a threefold title: Aredvi–Sura–Anahita. The names mean the "Moist One," the "Heroic One," and the "Immaculate One," respectively. It is interesting to note that these three forms correspond to the archaic Indo-European tripartite division of the pantheon and of human society into the three functions of the Farmer or Herdsman, the Warrior, and the Priest or Magician. Moistness is necessary to organic growth and fertility, heroism to the warrior class, and purity to the priests. Anahita is thus a great and all-encompassing goddess, much as Mithras had become a universal god-form.

Hekate

Hekate was originally a Thracian goddess. The Thracians were another Indo-European people who inhabited the region north of Greece in ancient times. She was sometimes merged with the goddess Artemis. Herodotus makes her the daughter of the Titans Perses and Asteria (both of whose names have to do with "shining light"). Hekate was a Moon goddess to begin with, but she was also associated with the Underworld. In the battle with the Titans, Hekate was an ally of Zeus, and so she remained an honored member of the Olympian community.

She can give humans riches, victory, and wisdom. As a goddess of the Underworld, she is known as the Invincible Queen and the goddess of enchantments and magic. She appears at crossroads accompanied by her pack of infernal hounds. Three-faced statues of her are often found at crossroads—where criminals were sometimes buried. On the eve of the full moon, offerings are made to these images.

Cybele

This goddess was originally the Phrygian Great Mother (Magna Mater) Goddess. The Phrygians were yet another Indo-European group from the Balkans close by the Thracians. Her Greek name means "of the cavern," and she seems to have been worshipped originally in mountaintop caves. She represents the savage, primitive forces of nature. In later times, she was merged with Rhea, the wife of Kronos and the mother of Zeus. She was also equated with Anahita— as were almost all "Great Goddesses." There is some good evidence to show that the cult of Cybele formed a politico-religious alliance with the Mithraists of Rome.

The comparative table below shows the relationships among the goddesses of various pantheons.

Iranian	Greek	Roman	Other
Anahita	Artemis	Diana	Cybele (Phrygian)
"		Minerva	
"		Fortuna	
Vanainiti	Nike	Victoria	
Spenta-Armaiti		Iuno	
	Hekate	Hecate	
	Ananke	Iustitia	
	Arete		

THE FINAL PERSECUTION

The divinities and the philosophy of Mithraism exerted a powerful social, political, as well as religious influence in the years just preceding the final decay of the Roman Empire. The famous quote of Ernest Renan, "If Christianity had been halted in its growth by some mortal illness, the world would have been Mithraist," has been rightly criticized. Mithraism was never intended to be a "popular religion" in the way Christianity was designed to be. Of course, it can be said that neither were the original teachings of Jesus the *magos* intended to be the basis for a religion suitable for the masses, but the times were ripe for just such a dogmatic "popular" faith of salvation through exaggerated promises, simple ritual, minimal work, and emotive faith.

In the realm of the Mithraea, Roman class distinctions were subordinated to initiatory authority. Masters and slaves were initiated side by side—often with slaves (or former slaves) becoming the religious authorities over their former masters. However, Mithraism remained closely tied to the old guard of the Roman Empire. It was well represented in the administration of the civil as well as military branches of the imperial government. Mithraists were known for their steadfast loyalty to the emperor and to the empire. This stands in stark contrast with how the Christians of the time thought.

After about three hundred years of initial failure, the church, as a corporation, began to be increasingly successful in political affairs. One of the chief elements in the church's propaganda war against other philosophies and faiths was imitation, while the other element was coercion. Both elements continued to be used throughout the history of Christianity. Features would be adopted from other faiths, and then when these features were later confronted by the Christians they would be attacked as blasphemous mockeries of Christian practices. This was just one of the techniques used to combat Mithraism. One of these instances will suffice to illustrate the point. The birthday of Mithras was universally celebrated on December 25. In the early years of Christianity, the birth of Jesus was hardly observed at all. But as the church corporation needed to fill out a liturgical calendar and co-opt as many of the rival celebrations as possible, they conveniently picked that day as the "birth day of Christ." If we are to believe the Bible concerning the historical circumstances of the birth of Jesus, then he must have been born in March, not December. This is because it was in March, at the time of the Roman New Year at the spring equinox, that the census was taken for purposes of the Caesar's tax collection. This is why Mary and Joseph supposedly had to come out of Egypt to be counted in Bethlehem, their original home city. The placement of Christmas on December 25 appears to have been nothing more than a ploy of the early church to obliterate an important pagan holiday. This had the added advantage of making it possible, after only a few generations had gone by, for the Christians to be able to accuse the pagans of putting their holidays on Christian holy days and thereby diabolically mocking them!

In 391 CE, Christianity became the official state religion of the Roman Empire, and all other cults were banned. Leading up to this final development, there were widening persecutions of the Mithraists by increasingly authoritarian forces within the church. At this point the element of coercion was put into full force. In 371, Mithraists were accused of being involved in an anti-imperial plot, and many were put to death. Christian mobs began to storm the Mithraea and burn and loot them. In 377 a Roman prefect named Gracchus who converted to Christianity offered as proof of the sincerity of his conversion that he would destroy a Mithraic temple. Often the Mithraic priests were killed and walled up inside the subterranean temples—their dead bodies left as a way to defile the sacred enclosure.

Many Mithraists themselves walled up the entrances to the Mithraea. They believed that the insane persecutions of the now victorious Christians would pass and more tolerant times were just around the corner. They would wait to no avail—until recently, at least!

For more than four hundred years Mithraism was present in the religious and philosophical life of the Roman Empire. Several emperors were primarily Mithraic in their religious orientations, including Caligula, Commodus, and Julian the Apostate. By 382 all official support for the Mithraic religion was withdrawn as all religious toleration was on the verge of extinction in a soon to be officially Christian "Roman" Empire.

THE MITHRAIC SYNTHESIS

Many Mithraic concepts were absorbed readily into the great pagan Alexandrian synthesis known as Hermeticism. The Magian and/or Mithraic traditions of Iranian religious thought were the main conduits for the transformative entry of those ideas into the religious and magical traditions of the West. After all, it is not insignificant that the very word *mageia* was borrowed from this ideology! But other traditions that informed Hermeticism (Israelite, Babylonian, Egyptian, and Greek) also, in turn, influenced and informed Mithraism as it evolved. Hermeticism was largely a phenomenon local to certain Hellenized population centers in the eastern Mediterranean (especially in Egypt), and was largely dependent upon written documents to preserve and spread its doctrines. This is why we know so much about it today, because many of these documents survived in the dry atmosphere of the Egyptian desert. Mithraism, on the other hand, was diffuse throughout the Western world (although it was decidedly not present on the Greek peninsula itself) and was spread through a vast system of living oral tradition. As the adherents of the tradition died, or were killed off, the chain of tradition was broken.

The ruins of magnificent subterranean Mithraic temples, called Mithraea, are scattered throughout Europe. Since each Mithraeum could only serve up to one hundred participants, and once there were more than that number a new Mithraeum had to be established, the spread of the cult was kept vigorous and vital. This spread and establishment cannot be denied or diminished in importance because it is deeply etched into the archaeological record.

Mithraism was overwhelmingly a cult of the military. However, it was not exclusively a cult of soldiers: merchants, civil servants, and even slaves were counted among its members. Although only a very few women are mentioned as being part of these Mysteries, in the East (Parthian Empire) they appear to have been accepted. In the last centuries of Mithraism's history, most of these men were soldiers or former soldiers in the Roman army. This is why so many Mithraea exist along the northern border of the empire, which was constantly under threat from Germanic tribes. However, it is important to point out that many Germanic tribes became part of the empire along the Rhine and Danube—where some of the most important Mithraea are found. It is also true that many individual Germanic tribesmen entered the Roman army, served their twenty years, and often returned to their homes north of the *limes* ("frontier"). It is interesting to note that there was a great number of Germanic tribesmen mentioned in the list of nationalities of the soldiers in the Roman army of Valerian captured by the Persian emperor Shapur the Great after the Battle of Edessa in 260 CE.

A sometimes overlooked aspect of Mithraism is that it functioned in a way similar to Freemasonry in modern Europe. It was an institution in which men of various nationalities and a wide range of social and economic standing could belong to the same group and communicate with one another in a meaningful way. In extreme cases, as noted previously, slaves could even be the initiatory masters of wealthy men.

Mithra had functioned as a deity who held fighting men together under an oath of loyalty and trustworthiness in exchange for success in battle and protection in society at least since the Achaemenid period in Persia. The figure of Mithra(s) simply continued much of this function under the guise of his Romanized cult as well. The god was a powerful agent for the bonding of men from various ethnic backgrounds, as well as diverse political and economic levels, into a single community—loyal to each other and to the Roman Empire. This was no insignificant function in a time when the empire was undergoing tremendous stress of every kind.

In the centuries during which it was active, Mithraism was perhaps the single most powerful agent in both synthesizing and disseminating ideas that we now identify as "magical" or "Hermetic" in Western Europe. Its importance is often ignored because it has left no direct continuous legacy or written records and because its own original homelands were eventually overrun by Islam.

The Roman form of Mithraism appears to have been the guiding factor in the early shaping of the system of Arcana—a series of iconic images—which eventually developed into the tarot as we know it. This cult was itself a synthesis of Iranian Magianism (Mithraism proper), Greek and Roman Stoicism, Babylonian astrology, and Greco-Egyptian Hermeticism. All of the magic and mystery of the Iranian system were synthesized in the scientific spirit of the Stoics and fused with Roman pragmatism to form a unique mystery religion with a warrior's soul.

The Mithraism practiced by fourth-century Roman soldiers along the Rhine was not the same exact religion practiced by second-century Roman citizens, and neither is the same system practiced by ancient Mithrists of Iran, the Caucasus, and Asia Minor. From the beginning, Mithraism was a syncretizing religion accepting elements from every symbolic system it met. This syncretization of outside elements was progressive, so there will be more extra-Iranian lore in the Roman codification (which includes the tarok imagery) than in the Greek codification with its twenty-four stoicheia. The constant factors in the Mithraic system appear to have been fixed by myth and by the initiatory grades with their teachings, as well as the iconography attached to these features.

CHAPTER 3

MAGIAN TEACHINGS
OF THE STOICHEIA

I t is certain that the earliest liturgical language of the Mithraists in the West was Greek. Portions of the Zarathustran *Gathas* are known to have been translated into that language in the Alexandrian period. The Greek ritual formulas were often interspersed with "barbaric" (Persian) words that apparently were not understood literally, although throughout the history of Mithraism its adherents took pride in the idea that their cult was *Persian* in origin. Inscriptions in the Mithraic cult sites were first in Greek, but soon after there was a shift to Latin (using the Roman script, of course). Therefore, to understand the earliest form of religio-magical classification of mysterious elements, we must understand the Greek system.

The Greeks call the letters of their alphabet *stoicheia* (στοιχεια), or "elements." This suggests the fact that they were thought to describe the building blocks of the *kosmos,* as well as act as a map for the understanding of that world order. This world order consists of twenty-four essential elements, or stoicheia, each of which finds manifestation in the twenty-four number/letters of the alphabet as bequeathed to mankind by Hermes.

The Greek writing system (which is still used to write the modern

Greek language) was developed over a course of time between ca. 1000 and 800 BCE as an adaptation of the Phoenician alphabet. The brilliant innovation of the Greeks was to create a purely phonetic script that accounted for all of the sounds of their language, both consonants and vowels. Their motive for doing so seems to have been entirely pragmatic. This system could be learned and used fairly quickly by clever people of all professions. Writing systems of antiquity tended to be extremely complex and cumbersome (e.g., Egyptian hieroglyphics or Mesopotamian cuneiform), a situation that was promoted so as to keep writing in the realm of a highly specialized and professional class. It was not that the ancients could not figure out how to write phonetically, it was simply that they did not want to make reading and writing easy.

Originally, the Greeks settled on a twenty-four-letter system. This number was probably arrived at for extra-linguistic reasons, since so many letters are not actually needed to represent the Greek language (double letters such as Ξ [= k + s] and Ψ [= p + s] were added, as were long versions of the "e" and "o"). This fixation on the number twenty-four may have been influenced by the number of phonetic characters in the Egyptian hieroglyphics.

The original system appeared as:

$$\text{Α Β Γ Δ Ε Ζ Η Θ}$$
$$\text{Ι Κ Λ Μ Ν Ξ Ο Π}$$
$$\text{Ρ Σ Τ Υ Φ Χ Ψ Ω}$$

As Sigurd Agrell points out, this system originally had numerical values simply applied 1–24. Later, in the second century BCE, a more advanced mathematical attribution of numbers was developed, but this was less important for magical or philosophical speculations than were the original and archaic numerical meanings.

In the chart above, what we call the "capital letter" forms were, in reality, the older epigraphical versions of the letters—that is, those used for making inscriptions in stone. The more cursive versions for writing on papyrus are the ones used to head the discussions of the stoicheia below.

Many readers of this book are probably already familiar with some of the mystical speculations surrounding the Hebrew letters in the Kabbalah. These traditions and those of the Mithraists were closely related, both in type and through historical connection.

The basic premise of the esoteric study of letters is that there is a hidden affinity between and among the following four aspects.

1. Number
2. Shape
3. Sound
4. Meaning

Furthermore, it is held that this correspondence extends from the realm of being or reality (the divine realm), whence it emanates, to the terrestrial realm. Each letter is a true symbol of a higher principle. That is to say, the letter is not a mere arbitrary sign of a principle, but is in fact a part, or manifestation, of it.

If the kosmos was created by means of the Word (an idea common to Judaic and Indo-European traditions) then the letters of the word(s) are actually the elements of the cosmic ordering.

By consciously absorbing the patterns inherent in the system of stoicheia, the Magian has the divine metagrammar to be able to be able to understand the self and the world in a way similar to the way the gods understand these things.

Number is over all and the highest of the aspects because it is nearest to divinity in its abstract quality. Number comes the closest to describing the element in its purest form. Knowledge of the numerical science, or arithmosophy, is primary because the ancient Hermetics, with the Pythagoreans, thought of number as the root (*archē*) of all things. In this they have been proved correct when it comes to the manifestation stage of existence. Every manifest thing can be quantified on many levels, from its dimensional measurements to the atomic numbers of the physical elements that comprise it. If we have the numbers on something, we can create or re-create it in the physical world. If this is true in the world of five senses and three dimensions, how much truer is it in the subtler realms?

The shape and sound of a stoicheion exist on the same level and give physical manifestation to the element. These are what the senses can both see and hear of the manifestation of the element in question. For practical reasons these are the most potent magical tools for the implementation of the powers of the stoicheia. Most of what we see in the historical record of Hermetic magic as recorded in the magical papyri involves the use of the elements on this level—by writing out formulas and/or by speaking them audibly.

The meaning of a stoicheion is by far the most complex aspect—because it is so manifold and multileveled. But ultimately it is the meaning that is the most important aspect for working magicians. It is the meaning that they seek most of all, and it is through the meaning that the keys to operating with the stoicheia are to be discovered.

The stoicheia of the Hellenistic Greeks were used by a variety of sects and philosophies as metaphors for their teachings. What the Pythagoreans taught through the letters, and what the Gnostics saw encoded in them, might vary slightly or greatly. It appears most likely that it was the Mithraic school that most influenced the eventual development of the tarot, and so I will concentrate on what the Mithrists most likely taught concerning the stoicheia. A great deal of the information for this section is drawn from the Pahlavi text called the *Bundahishn* ("the Creation"). This book was last re-edited in the ninth century CE. Although it has been significantly reformed by orthodox Zoroastrian ideas, there is a great deal of the archaic pre-Zoroastrian system still in evidence.

Each letter, each "element," contains a mystery, Persian *râz*. It conceals this mystery behind the simplicity of its external forms, yet it reveals the mystery in the meanings of these very forms. There was probably an older system of encoding the Mithraic Mysteries in some Iranian symbols. The most likely key to this is to be found in the ordering of the *yazatas*, "gods" or "angels," contained in the thirty-day Persian calendar. Parts of it are obviously still reflected in the later systems derived from it, and we will delve in to this in some systematic detail in appendix A. This lore also makes up part of our discussion of individual Greek stoicheia. But it is in the Greek system that Sigurd Agrell was able to discern some of the oldest aspects of the Mithraic system as such.

We know that later there was a twenty-two-letter system of Roman oracular usage, although no written account of this system seems to have survived. Agrell attempted to reconstruct this tradition, or at least one version of it, which he saw as part of Mithraic practice. It is noteworthy that we do have a surviving example of Greek letter-based oracular practice. This system is discussed in appendix B and examples from it sometimes make up part of the commentary on the stoicheia below.

In what follows we see the Hellenistic synthesis of Greek, Iranian, Judaic, and Egyptian lore. This same synthesis is what gave rise to what we now call the Hermetic tradition, as well.

α
alpha = 1

The first letter is emblematic of the primeval bull sacrificed by Mithras to engender the natural world of plants and animals. In the Semitic system, as reflected in the Hebrew *alef-bet,* the name of the first letter means "ox." This further solidified the idea that the first element was a bovine, since during the last centuries BCE, when the Magians were in close contact with the Semites of the Middle East, there was a great deal of cultural exchange between the keepers of the Judaic and the Magian secrets. In the Olympian oracle, *alpha* signifies that the questioner receives knowledge from god (Gk. θεος) that success, literally "good-fortune" (Gk. ευτυχως), can be expected in all things.

β
beta = 2

Agrell, preceding from a Zurvanite position, identifies the second element with "the demonic" and connects *beta* to the "evil god" Ahriman, who in the Zoroastrian system is responsible for the "evil creation." In Zurvanite doctrine, Ahriman is the second son of Zurvan/Aion, "evil" is the second principle of life, Angra Mainyu (= Ahriman) is called "the Second," and in the ancient Iranian cosmological text *Bundahishn* it is said that the cosmic whore Jahi relates her deeds *twice,* to the joy of Angra Mainyu.

However, it must be borne in mind too that the Mithrists were not the strict dualists they were sometimes assumed to be by certain scholars in the past. This is why Mithras can even on occasion be identified with Ahriman. It is also possible that the names Ahriman and Airyaman ("member of the tribe") became confused among outsiders. In strict dualistic Manicheanism, and in Gnosticism, the creator of the natural world is identified as the "Evil One." Of course, world creation is precisely the function of the bull sacrifice of Mithras! *Beta* therefore can be seen as an esoteric sign of Mithras himself in his function as the cosmogonic sacrificer and true magician. The Magian priests practiced animal sacrifice, whereas this became an unnecessary thing in more philosophically based Zoroastrianism.

γ

gamma = 3

The third letter is also a sign of the god Mithras. This time, however, in a transformed, triadic manifestation. Mithras is often called *triplasios,* the "Thrice-as-much," in Greek texts.

The goddess Anahita (Anaitis), the consort of Mithra (Mithras), also has a triple aspect: she is called Aredvi–Sura–Anahita (= "the Moist," "the Heroic," "the Immaculate"). These correspond to the three levels of ancient Iranian (and Indo-European) society and theology: fertility (farmers), war (warriors), and intellect (judges/priests). This is the true and most ancient origin of the triplicity of the Great Goddess.

In Christian mythology, much of which has been drawn from Iranian belief, there are three magoi, or Magians ("Wise Men," *not* "Kings") who visit young Jesus. This is symbolic of the Magian influence on the formation and perhaps even early education of that magician and teacher.

In the discussion of the tarok icons in chapter 4, we will discover that the various god-forms of the Iranians (as well as other Indo-European peoples such as the Greeks, Romans, Thracians, Phrygians, and so on) had three aspects, or hypostases, that described their complete natures. This "three-ness," or triplicity, is the mystery of this stoicheion.

δ

delta = 4

In Mithraic teachings the fourth letter is symbolic of the four natural elements—fire, air, water, and earth. These are represented in Mithraic art in the form of the four horses pulling the solar chariot, or quadriga, of Mithras.

The fourth yazata in the system of the Iranian calendar is Khshathra Vairya, "Sovereign Kingdom." This refers to the power to rule, and the corresponding line from the Olympian Oracle states: "Power (Gk. δύναμις), ill-timed, is customarily weak."

ε

epsilon = 5

The fifth stoicheion is connected to the personification of the primal fire, or spiritual force, embodied in Aion-Zurvan. Aion is the progenitor of the four natural elements embodied in the fourth stoicheion. The pentagram is the symbol of Aion.

Aion

In the Pahlavi *Bundahishn* we find it said that five forms of fire were created. The fire must also be tended five times a day, which forms a division of the day for sacred purposes. *Epsilon* is sometimes identified with the Light, or fiery spirit, in Hermetic teachings. This is the fire of Zurvan-Aion, which in Mithraic art is so often depicted coming out of Aion's mouth and entering the sacred altar fire (Atar).

ζ

zeta = 6

The number six is connected with sacrificial offerings in Mithraism. Six loaves of sacrificial bread were typically offered at the altar. The ancient Persians had six sacrificial festivals in the year. In Mithraism the number six was emblematic of the Moon, which was the sixth sphere of heaven, and referred to as the "provider."

η

eta = 7

The seventh element is symbolic of luck and happiness. Seven is the lucky number of the ancient Persians. Especially the Roman Mithraists had great regard for the number seven as it belonged to Mithras in his aspect as "the friendly helper" (*ho mesitēs*). The seventh month of the ancient Persian calendar was dedicated to Mithras, and the seventh sphere of heaven belonged to the Sun. Clearly also there are seven degrees in the Mithraic initiatory system, keyed to the seven visible planets. Seven is the number of the Amesha Spentas, the Holy Immortals.

θ

theta = 8

This is identified with the eighth sphere of heaven—the *primum mobil* of the fixed stars beyond the realm of the planets. This is thought to be a surface made of an icy substance and is referred to as the crystal-heaven. It is not the stars themselves (that is the fourteenth stoicheion) but rather the matrix in which they are fixed. This element contains the mysteries of the cosmological schemata, which includes the peculiar Mithraic form of astrology. This form of astrology has little to do with the natural world but is thought to be a more perfect metaphor for the psychic or spiritual reality.

ι

iota = 9

The ι stoicheion is the equivalent of the number nine and is connected with the abstract goddess of fate, or better put, Necessity—Ananke. She was especially honored among the Mithrists and was identified with the aether and the night. She belongs to the sphere of being beyond the fixed stars and planets. Her throne is said to be both above and below these regions. She is a driving force in initiates' need to attain higher grades of sanctification and to alleviate their own suffering and alienation.

κ

kappa = 10

Ten and multiples of ten are used in Iranian tradition to indicate death and misfortune. In the *Bundahishn* it is said that Angra Mainyu sent one thousand murderous demons (daêvas) upon the "Pure Man," and the evil god created ten thousand types of diseases. The Greek Olympian oracle connects this letter with the Greek word *kuma* (κύμα), meaning "wave" or the swell of the ocean, which is identified as something that is difficult to struggle against.

λ

lambda = 11

In the *Bundahishn* (ch. X) it is related that from the five members (the four legs and the penis) of the sacrificed cosmic bull sprang fifty-five types of grains and twelve types of healing herbs. Agrell points to the fact that $55 = 11 \times 5$ and determines that the original number signifying growth and vegetative vitality was the number eleven. The eleventh day of the Avestan-Persian calendar is dedicated to the Sun.

$$\mu$$

mu = 12

Twelve is the number of the healing herbs mentioned in chapter 10 of the *Bundahishn*. These sacred plants are the most powerful of the vegetative cosmos that spring from the marrow substance of the sacrificed bull. The twelfth day of the Avestan-Persian calendar is dedicated to the Moon, and it is in the Moon that the seed of the bull is purified and from this the many species of animals are derived.

$$\nu$$

nu = 13

The thirteenth letter is connected with the Helleno-Thracian goddess Hekate, who was given great honor by the ancient Mithrists. She is the chthonic goddess worshipped beside Ahriman-Pluto. Among the Greeks, Hekate was sometimes called Persia (or Perseie), which many believed was her name because she was thought to be a Persian goddess.

In a magical papyrus (*PGM* IV.2714) that describes an operation for love that is to be performed on the thirteenth or fourteenth night of the month, Hekate is invoked with many of her aspects. These include a being called the "arrow shooter." She is magically identified with Diana-Artemis and Aphrodite.

The thirteenth day of the Persian month is dedicated to the astral divinity Tishtrya (= the star Sirius) and was identified by Mithraic astrologers with Hekate.

$$\xi$$

xi = 14

Because of a longstanding structural need to have a sequence of symbols signifying the three main astral phenomena—fixed Stars, Sun, and Moon—and because the Sun and Moon symbols follow *xi*, Agrell concluded that the fourteenth letter of the alpha-beta was to be identified with the fixed stars in general (see *Bundahishn*, ch. IV).

It is most likely that the secret doctrine of Mithraism actually identified this symbol specifically with the stars of the constellation of the Bull (Taurus). In the Avestan (Persian) calendar, the fourteenth day of the month is holy to "the Soul of the Bull" (Av. *Gôshûrvan*).

O
omikron = 15

Mithraic teachings apparently connected the element *omikron* to the Sun, or the Light of the Sun. In chapter 15 of the *Bundahishn,* it is stated that the first men were created when Samaritan (or Gâyomart) died and left behind his semen, which was purified and activated by the revolving Sun. After forty years, the first humans arose—from a fifteen-leafed bush, each having the appearance of a fifteen-year-old girl. The fifteenth day of the month is sacred to the god of light, Ohrmazd.

π
pi = 16

The sixteenth element is to be identified with Mithras himself. In the Hermetic system, this belongs to another invincible god, Serapis. The sixteenth day of the Avestan month is dedicated to Mithras. Sometimes a sixteen-rayed star appears in conjunction with the inscribed name of ΜΕΙΘΡΑΣ.

ρ
rho = 17

According to the *Bundahishn* (ch. XXI), there are seventeen different forms of fluids—for example, the fluids of plants, the semen of animals and men, blood, sweat, tears, milk, and so on. These fluids are the embodiments of the vital forces of life in plants and animals. These are mingled during the growth process in physical existence.

The Avestan-Persian god Sraosha, brother of Mithra, carried the bundle of branches called the *baresman.* This bundle of twenty-one twigs or metal wires must be held by the Magian priest while officiating at sacrifice. He rules over and promotes the life forces of the world. It is these branches that belong to this element. They signify the ability of the Magian to bridge the gap between getik and menog, the material and spiritual worlds.

This stoicheion can also be related to one aspect of the Great Goddess, Anahita, who is mentioned more fully under *gamma* above. Here it is one of those tripartite aspects, Aredvi, which means "the Moist" that she belongs. She is consistently linked to bodies of water, especially great rivers.

σ

sigma = 18

The number eighteen is sacred to the gods of the Underworld and the realm of the dead. In the Avestan-Persian calendar the eighteenth day is dedicated to Rashnu, the second brother of Mithra and judge of the souls as they come to cross the Chinvat Bridge. In his role as a psychopomp, a conductor of the souls of the dead, Rashnu in many ways corresponds to the Hermes of the Greeks. Agrell also points out that this number, in his Uthark system, corresponds to the e-rune (ᛗ, *ehwaz*, "horse") and that in Germanic tradition this creature is seen as a transporter of the dead between the worlds.

τ

tau = 19

The microcosm of the human being is contained in the nineteenth element, because in it are found the twelve signs of the zodiac as well as the seven planets (12 + 7 = 19). In Babylonian tradition, nineteen was the number of man. By extension this would also be a number corresponding to the macrocosm, given the widely held idea that the macrocosm and the microcosm are structurally the same.

In the *Bundahishn* (ch. XXX) it is stated that "in fifty-seven years" (of the rulership of Saoshyant) all the dead will be resurrected. This is not a prediction but instead a mathematical/structural formula for transformation: 57 = 3 × 19. In the most ancient Indian mythic text, the *Rig Veda,* it is told how the cosmic man Parusha was sacrificed and the world made out of twelve parts of him (*RV* 10:90, 12–14). The next strophe mentions that "seven enclosing sticks" and "thrice seven fuel sticks" were used in the sacrificial ritual.

This element can be identified with the *Anthrōpos* (or *Logos*) of Hermetic cosmology.

Most powerfully, in the Avestan-Persian calendar the number nineteen corresponds to the fravashis—the souls of *individual* human beings—which are destined for perfection and ultimate resurrection in immortal Final Bodies.

υ
upsilon = 20

Chapter 7 of the *Bundahishn* has to do with the creation of the water. There we read how two main streams of primal water (called Rangha and Vanguhi) gave rise to eighteen rivers (i.e., 2 + 18 = 20). Therefore the number twenty is connected to the element of water. In Platonic thought too this seems to have been the case, because to that element Plato ascribes the geometrical model of the icosahedron—a twenty-sided solid. All of this is just fuel for the more popular correspondence between *upsilon* and water, because the Greek word for "water," ὕδορ, begins with that letter.

φ
phi = 21

The Avestan calendar dedicates the twenty-first day of the month to the masculine god of fertility and virility, Rama Hvastra. The correspondence between this tradition and the fact that the Greek word for the male sexual member, *phallos,* begins with this letter/number strengthens the connection between these concepts. The number twenty-one is the number of *connection:* there are twenty-one words in the most powerful *manthra* in Zoroastrianism, the Ahunvar, and there are twenty-one twigs or strands of wire that make up the *barsom* (Av. *baresman*), the symbolic tool by which the Magian makes connection between the material and spiritual worlds.

χ
chi = 22

Agrell tried to connect this stoicheion with the twenty-second letter of the Hebrew/Semitic alef-bet (= *taw*), noting that the chief meaning of this letter had to do with property and ownership. Both have as their original shapes a simple cruciform sign, either + or x. The shape in question was often a part of the design of early minted coins. But perhaps more important, and more graphically potent, is the suggestion that the cruciform sign refers to the southern, northern, eastern, and western winds referenced in the twenty-second sirozah of the Avestan-Persian calendar in a manthra dedicated to the yazata named Vata.

ψ
psi = 23

The twenty-third day of the month in the Avestan calendar is dedicated to the god of light and heaven—Ohrmazd. This stoicheion was also associated with Zeus or Jupiter-Caelus. The Mithrists called this god Zeus-Oromasdes (= Zeus-Ohrmazd). The shape of the grammaton might be suggestive of the bundle of lightning bolts often seen in Mithraic art, also referred to in the discussion of the twenty-third field of the Pergamon disk in appendix C.

ω
omega = 24

As the last stoicheion, as the fulfillment of the entire row of stoicheia, and therefore symbolic of the fulfillment of any series of things, the twenty-fourth element is indicative of richness or full power. Agrell sees a trinity of Iranian goddesses in this slot: Ashi Vanguhi (= Good Wealth), Daêna (= Insight or True Religion), and Cista (= Wisdom).

If we follow the first twenty-four days of the Persian-Avestan calendar, we see a process that ends in the enlightenment of the individual by being endowed with the most precious of gifts: Insight (Daêna). With a minimum of speculation, we could see that the adaptation of the twenty-four stoicheia to the Iranian system of symbols would go through the progression we have just witnessed. Also, on the basis of this, material qualities could be assigned to each of the stoicheia that would make them useful in divinatory practice. Each evokes some image; this image then becomes a key to a mystery.

The overwhelming classificatory use of Greek letters in religious systems of antiquity cannot be overlooked. Even the oldest manuscripts of the Hebrew Bible use Greek letters as numbers to signify the chapters and verses. However, it must also be noted that according to Franz Cumont, at least some of the Magians of Asia Minor were, in fact, using Aramaic as their ritual language as early as 500 BCE.[1] In such a case, it is also possible that there was an earlier classification of initiatory and cosmological images based on the key number of twenty-two (the number of letters in the Aramaic as well as Hebrew alef-bet). This would, however, have been perhaps most directly influenced by non-Jewish "pagan" Semitic lore of the Aramaeans.

It should also be recognized that the Roman alphabet was adapted to the older lore surrounding the Greek and Aramaic (or Hebrew) letters. This was especially true when it came to the use of the Roman letters as esoteric numerical codes. Evidence connected with the famous SATOR-ROTAS square clearly indicates that the Roman letters were used in numerology and that the mythic system used to encode this square was Mithraic. In a monograph titled "The Mithraic Origins and Meanings of the Rotas-Sator Square," Walter O. Moeller showed that when the numerical equivalents of each of the Roman letters of the SATOR square is added up, it equals the value of the addition of all of the names of the seven Mithraic initiatory grades—that is, 2,520. This formula is presented in more detail in the discussion of the symbolism of Kronos, the tenth Arcanum, in chapter 4. As a matter of fact, this sum also just happens to be the equivalent of 7×360, or the number of things (such as the Mithraic grades, planets, Greek vowels, and so on) times the number of degrees in a circle (= Aion-Zurvan). Such meaningful coincidences may serve no other purpose than to cause those who discover them, or those who gaze upon them, to stand in awe of the Mystery itself. If this is so, it has served a fine purpose.

There is another important piece of hard evidence for the twenty-four-fold character of the divinatory symbol system widely used in Hellenistic times. This is the so-called magic disk of Pergamon, and it is the subject of appendix C.

CHAPTER 4

THE MAGIAN TAROK

ROMAN ADAPTATION

Although the Mithraism and Magianism of the Hellenistic period was originally couched in a purely Iranian idiom (third to second century BCE), with its symbols a syncretic mixture of Iranian and Chaldean forms, it spent much of its history being assimilated in the West (mainly in Asia Minor) within the Hellenistic, Greek-based, symbology. This occurred in the first century BCE and extended into the early years of the Christian era. It was then that it came into contact with the general mixture of symbols we call "Hermetic." But as the power of Rome and things Roman came to dominate the Mediterranean world and Europe as a whole, and as more and more citizens of the empire became attracted to and joined in the Mithraic cult, the Hellenism of its symbology gave way to an increasing degree of Latinate characteristics. The Latinate base was made indispensable because the cult was to spread among the population of the western empire whose lingua franca was (vulgate) Latin. Vulgate Latin was the language spoken by the common person in the empire. This form of Latin was in many regards simplified from the classical standard, and from it would arise the Romance languages (e.g., Italian, French, Portuguese, Spanish, and Romanian). It is the hidden genius of syncretic religious and magical systems that they can maintain their existences while in a constant state of change and evolution—and all this without giving up their aura of stability and ancient tradition.

The chief effect of this phenomenon for our study was the fact that the Greek language, which had earlier replaced the Iranian as the liturgical or ritual language of the Mithraic Mysteries, was itself replaced by Latin. When this happened the former power of the Greek *alphabeta* to classify and order the symbols of the Mysteries in an instructive way was greatly diminished. The response to this appears to have been to use the Roman alphabet to reorder and reinterpret the initiatory and cosmological data taught in the Mysteries. Also, as Latin (often of a vulgate dialect) was the common language of citizens of the Roman Empire, it was a language that brought people of various nationalities together. This was also a function of the Mithraic cult itself.

It would be untenable to speculate that there was a system of tarot cards going back into a time period well beyond the age of the Renaissance in Italy (and beyond the time of the printing press!). What is being posited is that there was a more archaic system of symbols, keyed to definite sequences such as the Iranian/Zoroastrian sirozahs, the Greek letters (stoicheia), the Roman letters (Lat. *litera* or *nota*), and perhaps even Germanic runes and Egyptian hieroglyphic phonetic signs. These form the deep background of the icons that came to be the final sequence of images known as the tarot in the fifteenth century. It is possible that each of these simple signs carried with them an oral verbal tradition, which explained the signs in iconographical terms. Such a tradition certainly survives in the form of the Germanic rune poems, which provide "word pictures" that could easily be translated into representational images very similar to those that became the tarot. So the original icons would probably have been mnemonic mental images keyed to divinities or letters of an alphabet used in divinatory operations. Only much later were these mental images actually translated into pictorial representations.

THE ROMAN SYSTEM

The Greek alphabeta has twenty-four stoicheia, whereas the Roman system, as it was used in the Imperial period, had only twenty-three letters. But for magical or divinatory purposes the system used only twenty-two letters. This is because the letter *y* was never used as an initial letter. It was employed to transcribe the Greek letter *upsilon* when words were borrowed from that language into Latin. Thus, only twenty-two letters could be used for initial sounds in the Latin language. Since the divinatory practice seems to have been based on the drawing of lots (usually made of metal) with either the letters or short phrases beginning with these twenty-two letters, such lots (or *sortes* in Latin) could only have been twenty-two in number. Their order, as further shown in table 2 on page 166, is identical to that used in modern languages (with a few deletions for phonetic reasons) as follows:

A B C D E F G H I K L M N O P Q R S T V X [Y] Z

Note that /i/ took care of the sound [j] (which is really only a stylistic variant of the I), K was used in Greek loanwords, and V and [u] were identical. Thus, in classical Latin, the name "Julius" would have been written IVLIVS (and pronounced [YOO-lee-us]).

It therefore seems that the whole of the Hellenistic system of Mithraic esotericism, along with much of that which we have come to call Hermetic esotericism, was re-encoded from the Greek system into a Roman one. This new encoding probably dominated occult teachings in western Europe from about the second century CE into the medieval period. Greek maintained its position more firmly in the East. These variations in linguistic encodings are also reflected in the history of the exoteric religions, where Greek dominated in the East and Latin in the West.

The re-encoded system of the Roman esotericists based on the key number twenty-two is outlined in table 2 in appendix E (see page 166). An essential component of this table is, of course, the by now well-known tarot symbolism.

SYMBOLISM OF THE MAJOR ARCANA

It is most likely that certain simple iconic images (which would have also certainly found their way into some representational art of the day) were attached to the twenty-four stoicheia of the Greek alphabeta, and these images were evoked in the divinatory practices that employed the Greek letters in late antiquity. The images were probably only evoked in the imaginations of the readers, based on verbal descriptions that were part of the initiatory process. For the sake of brevity and utility, the images were merely suggested by the letters, with the process of suggestion triggered by a divinatory keyword and oracular phrase.

The scenario suggested by this history is that the tarot, as it surfaced in the late Middle Ages, was not the *beginning* but rather the *end* of a long process of development and transformation. There are a number of clues we can use to reconstruct the oldest imagery of the original Roman tauroc, which can, in turn, act as the basis for a possible recovery of the imagery of the two lost cards of the prototypical and hypothetical Greek taurok.

Below I present images of various sets of tarot cards to illustrate the iconography of the Arcana. Usually I use the oldest (almost) complete set of the Major Arcana from Renaissance Italy, known as the Visconti-Sforza deck (mid-fifteenth century), and the designs of the Gringonneur cards, which were supposedly produced for King Charles VI (mid-fifteenth century) but which experts assign a Venetian origin. The third example may be drawn from any one of a number of various decks. Sometimes this is the Marseilles deck of the mid-eighteenth century, upon which the most common modern occult designs have been based. The most well known of the modern decks is, of course, that of A. E. Waite produced under the guidance of the Golden Dawn symbolism as developed by S. L. MacGregor Mathers.

From a historical perspective, one of the most fascinating aspects of the study of these images is that the icons are drawn from such a wide range of sources. But we should not be surprised by this. Mithraic/Hermetic syncretism brought together elements from a wide number of sources and forged them into a coherent but ever evolving system. The cultural elements are also usually explicable historically. Whatever agent was responsible for putting first the Greek synthesis and subsequently the Roman synthesis of this material together used definite principles for doing so.

It will be noticed that many of the main elements are derived from the Iranian Mithraic (or Magian) stream of thought, or from the Semitic Mesopotamian tradition, or from Egyptian mythology and religion—as well as from the primary Greek and Roman traditions. But less well-known elements are also quite strongly represented. Old and suppressed, or officially ignored, gods and goddesses of Rome such as Orcus and Libera figure prominently, while Greek elements are often those that were imported at some time from originally non-Greek realms (such as Hekate from Thrace). The reasons for this openness to suppressed material is that the Mithraic and Magian tradition was falling increasingly into this category in the West itself. The Mithraic cult became a clearinghouse for all kinds of ideas being driven progressively more underground by the establishment of orthodox Christianity.

Another remarkable feature of the history of the images is the fact that often cards with a relatively late date of origin (e.g., the seventeenth or eighteenth century) may demonstrate clearly archaic characteristics that speak to a symbolism that has its origins in the Roman Age as much as 1,500 years earlier. This is possible only because the older cards, upon which the symbolism of the later ones was based, have disappeared. Even the Visconti-Sforza and Gringonneur decks survive only in fragmentary form. Most of the old cards from the early modern period have long since fallen to dust.

Of tremendous importance is also the designation "Arcanum" in relation to the tarot. The word is Latin for "secret" or "mystery." Its original meaning had to do with something that was closed off, separate from the profane world: an *arcanum* is something concealed from the mundane world. But the images referred to as Arcana at once both conceal and reveal meaning. It is striking that in the Germanic world signs that functioned in a way very similarly to the esoteric values of the Greek and Roman letters were referred to as *runes* in the native Germanic terminology—a word that means "mystery" or "secret."

From a structural perspective, the enumeration of the Arcana follows two lines. Each has an exoteric and an esoteric designation. The exoteric designation appears right after the letter designation, and the esoteric number appears in square brackets.

The interpretive comments offered on each of the tarok images below are drawn from a variety of sources, but they cannot claim to be exhaustive. This edition has been graced with the photographic artwork of Amber Rae Broderick, which seems to reach out over the centuries, encompassing not only the archaic world in which these icons had their genesis but also touches the early twentieth-century epoch in which the scholar and poet Agrell did his work. Readers are invited to review material found elsewhere in this book, especially where the symbolism of the magical disk of Pergamon or the lore of the individual Greek stoicheia are outlined, to discover for themselves hidden links between the Roman system of Arcana and some of the older traditions. The discovery of the Greek letter that corresponds to each of the Roman Arcana is often essential in reconnecting the Arcanum in question to the deepest levels of mystery.

Apis
The Fool
A = 1 [0] [1+4.1-4.3]

The general image of The Fool is that of what appears to be a court jester wandering in the countryside with a bundle on a stick. He is often being bitten on the leg or elsewhere by a dog. In the Gringonneur deck the man has the ears of a bull or some other animal. This is perhaps explained by the origin of the name of the image and the whole series of images discussed below.

The name (*Il Matto* in Italian and "The Fool" in English) is universal in its implications. Originally there were only three cards called "trumps": The Fool, The Magician, and The World. Each of these are worth five points in the game of Tarock. The word "trump" has its origin in the Latin word *triumphus* but was also influenced by the word *triumviri,* "three men." It was before these three men, the triumvirate, that the triumphal victory marches in Rome were made. In the symbolic language of the tarot, these three men were the human figures represented in the three cards in question, which came at the beginning and end of the sequence of images.

In fact, as mentioned earlier, the name of the whole system may stem from the original name for this, the first image. Agrell pointed out that the French Provençal word *taruc,* derived from the Latin *taurus,* "bull," means a "stupid person," a "bull-headed" person—a "fool." Even more evocative is the idea that the name of the whole system is derived from the Greek term for the Mithraic "bull slaying," ταυροκτόνος, which was later Romanized as *tauroktonia* (tauroctony). This act of bull sacrifice is, of course, responsible for the inception of the natural generative and regenerative universe; it is the beginning of all developing or evolving things. Therefore, from a Mithraic viewpoint, it is the beginning of the series of evolutionary and initiatory images, and a description of the whole series as well. This is much like naming a series of letters after its beginning: alpha-beta, ABC, fuþark, and so forth.

The original number of this image was one. The later assignation of the number zero to the image is a modern affectation. The number one, as a pure quality (not a quantity), contained most of the connotations zero has for the modern mind. Oneness contains everything and is therefore the virtual equivalent of nothing.

The Roman-Mithraic name of this image for divinatory purposes should be one that begins with an "A." This name would have been readily available to the Romans of the time in the form of the name of the Egyptian divine bull of the Sun: Apis. Apis was very well known in the ancient world. This is what Agrell assigned to the icon in question here. However, it is my thought that this word, Apis, contains a great mystery. The Latin word *apis* also means "bee." This is a symbol for the Mazmaga—the Great Fellowship of initiates responsible for spreading the philosophy of Zarathustra and for insinuating elements of it into other systems. The Fool is most often an (at first) unwitting initiate into this invisible realm of wisdom.

· The Fool ·

Image by Amber Rae Broderick

Gringonneur   Visconti-Sforza   Marseilles

The original image was probably that of the complete Mithraic bull slaying (tauroctony), although for divinatory purposes the image was probably no more than the horns of a bull, perhaps with a dog depicted below the horns. When we look at a complete depiction of the Tauroctony, we see Mithras stabbing the bull with a knife, while he is looking away—in disgust or ignorance of the consequences of his action—as a dog licks the blood dripping from the wound. A scorpion is stinging, and attempting to devour the bull's testicles, while below the whole scene slithers a snake, and above it hover images of the Sun and Moon, as well as the entire zodiac. This one scene prefigures many of the major images that underlie the tarok series.

It seems that the bull has been replaced by the human figure of the (bull-eared) jester, but it should be noted that the dog is connected in a similar way to both.

The original meaning of this image is cosmogonic. It is the beginning of all things, which is present in all things at all times. It is the primeval sacrifice that gives rise to all that exists. The active agent, the mind, the spirit (of God or Man) is, in the beginning, unaware of the consequences of these actions that set evolution and change into motion. This is why Mithras is looking away from his action in almost every scene of the Bull

The Tauroctony: Mithras Slaying the Bull

Sacrifice. It is not his conscious will to kill the bull, but he is forced by circumstance into doing so. But a greater good, previously hidden from him, is revealed through this act. This is why he is called the "Fool." All acts based on the exploration of the unknown, based on the impulse to satisfy curiosities about what is hidden, begin in Foolishness.

The name Agrell gave to this Arcanum, Apis, is somewhat problematic. It is the only name connected to Egyptian religion. Apis is the Greek and Roman name given to the Egyptian god Hapi-ankh, who was incarnated in a living bull with certain markings. When such a bull died, it was mummified and worshipped. On more than one occasion foreign conquerors of Egypt (including the Persians) sacrificed and ate the Apis Bull—much to the annoyance of the Egyptians. Such actions were certainly always foolish politically.

BACATUS
THE MAGICIAN
B = 2 [1]

Agrell is anxious to identify the second card with the concept of "the demonic." He demonstrates that there are many similarities between the image of the Magician or Juggler and that of the ancient Egyptian demon god Set (Σηθ). He notes, for example, that the human figure depicted on the second card is almost always carrying a magical staff or scepter. In the Greek magical papyri (*PGM* IV.180), Set-Typhon is called *skeptouche*, "scepter carrier." In *PGM* XXXVI (8ff.) there is even a drawn image of Set that looks very much like the typical depiction of the Magician in the tarot. In addition, the scepter of divine power (*uas*) carried by Egyptian gods is in the very image of the god Set.

In Egypt, Set was always considered to be the god of foreigners. When the Hyksos Semites ruled in Egypt (ca. 1700–1550 BCE) their Ba'al was identified with Set, and when the Persians ruled there (527–405 BCE) it is also likely that their Mithra (in his war-god aspect) was likewise identified with Set. Besides this, the thoughtful Magians resident in Egypt would have understood the myth of Set in a light quite different from that of many of the Egyptians of the time. They no doubt

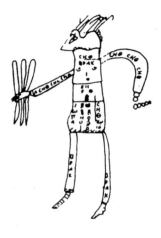

Image of Set-Typhon
from PGM XXXVI, 8ff.

would have seen in Set's killing and dismembering of the body of Osiris a reflection of their ancient cosmogonic myth wherein a sacrifice (either of a bull or cosmic man [Gâyomart]) gave rise to the world. This act of divine will over the cosmic order was the first creative magical act, and thus Mithras (or here Set) could be identified as the first true magician.

It should be recalled that the Egyptian god Set was not always considered to be some sort of devil. He is a defender of the gods in his martial aspect and was the chief god of some of Egypt's most illustrious and successful pharaohs: Seti I, Rameses II (the Great), Seti II, and Setnakht. I am sure many other pharaohs of the age were devotees of Set as well.

The oldest name of this image refers to the figure's function as a magician by describing him as "the one who carries a magic staff." The Italian name is *il bagatto*, while in French it is *le bateleur*. These names are both ultimately derived from the Latin *baculatus*, "one who carries a *baculum* (staff)," which here becomes *bacatus*, with the loss of the suffix *-ul*. Originally it did not refer to the more exalted magician but connoted a juggler, or one who deals in illusions. But this is in keeping with a certain philosophical or cosmological principle inherited from Indo-Iranian belief. The creator of the natural or sensible universe is a wielder of "illusion." It is in the stead of this god that magicians act when working their wills upon the natural universe to cause changes to occur according to their wills.

Image by Amber Rae Broderick

Rosenwald   Visconti-Sforza   Marseilles

The more usual modern name, The Magician, is of ultimate Iranian origin. It is derived from Latin *magus*, "magician," which was, in turn, derived from the Greek *magos* (with the same meaning). The ultimate origin of the word is Iranian *magû,* which designated a priest of the fire cult. Originally, this name belonged to a certain tribe or caste, but as time went on some of them began a westward migration and began to initiate outsiders into their mysteries. To differentiate these initiated practitioners of the Iranian tradition from other practitioners of Hermetic or other forms of Hellenistic magic, we call them Magians. For Arab Muslims, the word became a synonym for different kinds of infidels. For example, the Norsemen encountered by Arab travelers during the Viking Age were also called *majûs.*

The original meaning of this image was probably that of the magician, the primeval creator of the world according to will. Alternatively, it is the sorcerer, the one who is expert at deception. In the Iranian mythology, this may be exemplified by Ahriman, the second son of Zurvan-Aion. Some views have it that Mithras was identified with Ahriman at some stage, but this seems unlikely. The magician completes the twofold nature of the subject of initiation into the Mysteries of Mithras and represents the one who actually undergoes and experiences the mysteries of the initiations. The Fool is the natural part of the subject, and the Magician is the transcendental or psychic aspect.

The figure depicted in the image called The World constitutes the third aspect of the subject of initiation: the one being initiated.

All the images between these first two and the last one demonstrate the unfolding of the cosmos within the body and soul of the mystēs. These are paralleled in the myth of Gâyomart, the cosmic man, discussed in chapter 2 under "Mithraic Cosmology," page 27.

CAELIS
THE PAPESS OR THE HIGH PRIESTESS
C = 3 [2]

The oldest images of this Arcanum show a seated female figure wearing a crown, sometimes three-tiered, and perhaps holding a book. The

Visconti-Sforza version of this figure shows the crown surmounted with a crescent moon. This led Agrell to associate her with the Egyptian goddess Isis, who was often depicted with a crescent headdress in Egyptian art. A depiction of Isis would not seem to be far-fetched in an iconography having its origins in the twilight of the Roman Empire, since the cult of Isis was among the most popular of foreign cults at that time. But some scholars have argued that Isis was not likely to have been a part of Mithraic symbology because the two cults, that of Isis and that of Mithras, were in antagonistic competition with one another in the Roman period. This has, however, been proved incorrect—at least from the Mithraic side—as even a statue of Isis has been found in a Mithraeum in Rome.

As far as the name of the figure is concerned, the designation "High Priestess" seems to be a modern one. The older name was "The Papess" (French *La Papesse* and Italian *La Papessa*). The name was changed in some instances to appease the Catholic Church, which found the very word "Papess" heretical. The meaning of the name is clear. This is the Arcanum of the divine feminine in human life and form. To say "The Papess" is to say, "This is the highest form of the divine in the form of a human woman." She is the priestess of all the goddesses—especially those who are seen in triple form: Anaitis (Anahita), Hekate, and the Anatolian Magna Mater, Cybele.

In an archaic Roman context she would be the Virgo Maxima, who presided over the priestesses of Vesta in Rome. The Virgo Maxima would then be analogous to the male Pontifex Maximus, which is discussed under the Pope/Hierophant. As Virgins, the priestesses under the Virgo Maxima were in a liminal state of being between male and female and therefore exercised many social and religious powers otherwise reserved to men in Roman society. But their main sacred function was to keep the eternal flame of the City of Rome, its ritual hearthflame, ablaze. This eternal flame element would have struck a deep and resonant chord with the Iranian elements of Mithraism.

In the Mithraic context, it is one of the best-kept secrets that women, although not often initiated in the Mysteries of the seven grades of

Image by Amber Rae Broderick

Rosenwald   Visconti-Sforza   Marseilles

Mithraism, nevertheless played a part in the Mysteries and in the cultic life of the initiates as priestesses.

In later times, when Asian cults were streaming into the Roman Empire, no cult was more popular than that of the Egyptian goddess Isis. She was referred to with the honorific Latin title of Prima Caelitum, the "First of Heaven," which in a shortened form would be Caelis, the "Heavenly One." This, speculates Agrell, would be the original divinatory title of this Arcanum. Her original image might have been a female face or head surmounted by a crescent moon headdress or crown.

An alternate to this is provided by the name of the Phrygian goddess Cybele. It is known that the cults of Cybele and that of Mithras formed a strong alliance in Rome and that the cult of the Goddess in many ways formed the feminine side of Mithraism. Therefore, Cybele could also have been the name of this Arcanum.

Understanding of this Arcanum is provided by knowledge of, and experience in, the threefold nature of all divine things. The High Priestess is the representation of the abstract principle of triplicity.

DIANA
THE EMPRESS
D = 4 [3]

The old tarot cards universally show a regal woman seated on a throne, always holding, or otherwise associated with, a shield with a crest showing the image of an eagle, and sometimes she is also shown holding a scepter surmounted with a globe. These are traditional medieval and early modern symbolic attributes of imperial power. The Empress is empowered to rule the terrestrial realm (with her consort the Emperor).

The Roman goddess Diana most clearly answers to the meaning of the fourth Arcanum. No doubt it was her name under which the Arcanum was encoded. An early image of Diana, showing her to be the ruler of the four elements, depicts her head surrounded by the shapes of four emblematic animals: a salamander, an eagle, a quadruped, and a dolphin. Each represents an element: fire, air, earth, and

Image by Amber Rae Broderick

Rosenwald   Visconti-Sforza   Marseilles

Image of Diana and the Elements

water, respectively. Note too that the eagle present in this image is also a zoomorphic symbol that continued to be present in the iconography of The Empress until modern times.

"The Empress" is not the true name of this Arcanum, but rather its title. This is also true of the other Arcana. Diana is at least one of its true Roman names and most likely the most popular name for the Arcanum for divinatory purposes. It is tempting to identify this Arcanum also with the Persian name Daêna (= "Insight" or "True Religion"). This is one of the trinity of goddesses classified under the Greek letter *omega*.

Understanding of this Arcanum is provided by knowledge of, and experience in, the fourfold nature of all earthly things. The Empress is the representation of the abstract principle of fourfoldedness and the natural realm.

The scholar of Indo-European comparative religion Georges Dumézil points out that Diana combines in herself four realms.

1. The sky (her name is derived from the word for "open sky")
2. Continuity of the successions of time
3. Conferring of the *regnum* (kingship)
4. Patronage of births[1]

As the Papess or High Priestess is the Arcanum of the divine feminine in human form, the Empress is the Arcanum of the pure divine feminine in her numinous aspect.

EON
THE EMPEROR
$E = 5 \ [4]$

In most early images of The Emperor, he is shown seated on a throne holding a globe in his left hand and a scepter in his right. Often he is depicted with an eagle—not just the image of one but rather a representation of a live bird. This is seen in the Mantegna card called IMPERATOR VIIII (Emperor 9). The Mantegna card called IVPITER XXXXVI (Jupiter 46) shows an Emperor-like figure in a vesica piscis, standing on a sphere. In standard medieval iconography the ball symbolizes the secular world, while the scepter symbolizes sovereignty within it.

These symbols go back to a time long before the Middle Ages. In Mithraic iconography we see images of the leontocephalic (lion-headed) god that bear most of the important characteristics of the Emperor. Such images have been identified with the Iranian Zurvan, as well as the Greek Aion and Kronos. They usually show the god with the body of a man and the head of a lion (or, alternatively, with the physical form of a man with a lion's head on his chest), who stands on a sphere holding a scepter (or a variety of scepters). He also has either two or four wings, reflected in the presence of the eagle.

This lion-headed god is seen to rule over time and to hold governance over the movement of the stars. Ulansey has even interpreted the double equators circling the globe that the god stands on as symbolic of the precession of the equinoxes, the discovery of which he views as fundamental to Mithraic origins.

The globe that figures so prominently in the image of the Emperor is also widely present in images of Mithras, who is sometimes depicted holding the globe of the world. This globe is identified with the cosmic egg, out of which the order of the world emerged and to which it will return.

· The emperor ·

Image by Amber Rae Broderick

Gringonneur

Mantegna (ca. 1470)
(Imperator VIIII)

Mantegna
(Jupiter 46)

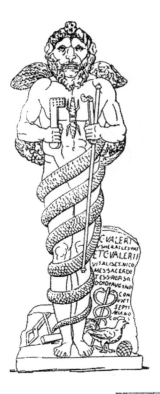

The Lion-Headed God

The Orphic Phanes

The title of this card is universally found in all the tarot packs. This is the Arcanum of the Ruler. In many Hellenistic cosmologies the spheres of existence surrounding the Earth are called *Aiōnes*, and over each of these levels of existence there is placed a Ruler, who is called an Archon. An *Aiōn* is both an extremely long duration of time (an "Age") and a spatial or dimensional concept. The Emperor is the Archon of Archons and is the archetype of Eternal Time itself. In Roman practice, Greek words beginning with /ai-/ were often Latinized by spelling them with a long /ē/, and thus *Aiōn* became *Eon,* which is the Latin title given to this Arcanum.

One can perceive the essential power of the rulership of Aion as the eclectic Magians of the first centuries of this era understood it in a passage from one of the Greek magical papyri, which reads in part:

> Who shaped the forms of the beasts (of the Zodiac)? Who found their routes? . . . What Aion feeding an Aion rules the Aions? One deathless god. Thou art the father of all and assign souls to all and control all, king of the Aions and lord. . . . By thy power the elements exist and all things come into being. . . . Thine is the eternal processional way (of heaven). . . .

Understanding of this Arcanum is provided by knowledge of, and experience in, the art and craft of rulership (or leadership). As the Empress is the power to rule in this world, the Emperor is the actual wielder of that power to rule.

Flamen
The Hierophant
The Pope
F = 6 [5]

The image of The Pope is almost universally consistent in all the early cards. We see a man seated on a throne, wearing sacred vestments, and holding a key in his right hand. Often he also has either a scepter or a book either in his other hand or on his lap. He always wears a crown, and in the Visconti-Sforza image this is a three-tiered affair. At first glance these symbols are immediately understandable in terms of medieval iconography: the book is the missal (or gospel) and the key is the key to the kingdom of heaven traditionally associated with St. Peter, of whom medieval legend has it that the Pope was the representative. The crown and scepter are symbols of the Pope's authority to rule.

But the preponderance of evidence presented throughout this book consistently points in the direction of these tarot images having their ultimate origins in a context well beyond the world of the medieval Roman Catholic Church. In fact, it seems that the imagery was purposefully manipulated at the time of the Renaissance to make it appear Catholic and thus be more acceptable to the religious authorities of the time. The church was apparently never fooled. It was later pressure from the church that caused more modern printers to change the names of the Papess and Pope to the High Priestess and Hierophant, respectively.

Iconographically, the image of the Pope again has much in common with the image of the leontocephalic god discussed and illustrated in our discussion of The Emperor above. Especially conspicuous are the presence of the symbols of the key and scepter.

The name or title of the card, *Il Papa,* refers, of course, to the popular medieval title of the Bishop of Rome, the head of the Roman Catholic Church. In the period of gradual transition from paganism to Christianity, the Pope had, in fact, taken for himself the title of the high priest of the official religion of pagan Rome—the Pontifex Maximus (the "Greatest Bridge-Builder"). The bridge in question is that link or connection between the world of the divine or of the ancestors (*maiores*) and that of terrestrial life. The more generic term for a *pontifex* was *flamen,* "priest," a word that, in fact, derived from the same root as the name of the Vedic priest: Brahman. It would then be from this title, Flamen, that this Arcanum would take its name.

Looking back into the Magian context, we see that this is the Arcanum of the official priestly *magû,* or *atharvan.* In the divine world,

Image by Amber Rae Broderick

Gringonneur   Visconti-Sforza   Mantegna (Papa X)

this function is associated with Sraosha, the brother of Mithra and the patron of officiating priests. This function is also sometimes ascribed to Ahriman, the god of darkness.

The title Papa comes from the child's word for "father," or *pater*. This is, of course, the name of the highest level in the Mithraic series of grades. In this Arcanum we see the link between "fatherhood" and "priesthood."

Understanding of this Arcanum comes from knowledge of, and experience in, the linkage between the world of the divine and the world of humanity. The Latin word *religio,* from which the English word *religion* directly comes, literally means "re-connection." The craft of the true priest is to reconnect the worlds of gods and humans.

In many ways the Pope is closely related to the Emperor. Both are symbols of the divine masculine. The Emperor is a representation of this on a higher, archetypal level, while the Pope (or Hierophant) represents this power as expressed in terrestrial life.

The Pope and Emperor form a masculine pair of terrestrial and celestial representations of the divine that structurally answer to the Papess and Empress in the feminine realm.

GAUDIUM
THE LOVERS
G = 7 [6]

The Gringonneur card shows three couples (a total of six persons) with two Cupids shooting arrows at them. The Visconti-Sforza card shows a man and a woman seated with a single blindfolded ("love is blind") figure of Cupid hovering above them, about to hurl his arrow downward. Cupid also holds in his left hand a thin scepter—signifying his power to rule in matters of love. An archetype of the tarok card may be provided, certainly in spirit, by the Mantegna card depicting VENVS (43). It shows the goddess of love bathing in the sea or in a stream, with her son, Cupid, standing behind her, blindfolded and carrying bow and arrow. In front of the goddess stand three young girls grouped closely together. The iconography is highly reminiscent of Botticelli's famous

·The Lovers·

Image by Amber Rae Broderick

Gringonneur   Visconti-Sforza   Mantegna (Venus 43)

magical-allegorical painting *Primavera* (usually called in English the "Allegory of Spring").

In Botticelli's Neoplatonic allegory, Venus and Cupid are placed in the center of a process by which natural forces are transmuted to spiritual or intellectual ones. To the right of the painting we see Zephyr, the West Wind, pursuing the Nymph of Spring (Chloris), whom he impregnates with carnal desire. She is thereby transformed into Flora. At this point in the process the spirit of divine love enters. It is provided by Venus (who presides over the whole process) and Cupid, who shoots his arrow into a group of three young girls—who represent the Three Graces: Castitas (Chastity), Pulchritudo (Beauty), and Voluptas (Passion). This part of the image has been interpreted as the initiation of Chastity into the fullness of Beauty and Passion. At the far left of the painting is Mercury, god of intelligence, dispelling the clouds that veil reason. This is the key to the identity of the three women in the Mantegna card, and in a large sense the key to the understanding of this Arcanum.

The origin of the Cupid figures obviously lies not in Christian but rather in pagan mythology. It was in this form that the Greek god Eros was depicted. His bow and arrow are symbolic of the ability of *eros,* love, to act over long distances. Really this action can take place through various dimensions of reality—or, to use terminology more contemporary with the image, from one sphere to any other. The power of attraction between one body and another, be that between two human beings, or between a human and a god, is essential in the initiatory process.

As is true with all the other cards, the title popularly given to it in later times is a simplistic description of what is visible or apparent in the depiction. The real name of the image was kept secret and hidden. That name was Gaudium, "delight," or "the source of delight." The simplistic title "The Lovers" focuses only on what is seen or obvious, whereas the name Gaudium focuses on the entire process at work in the Arcanum.

From a numerological perspective, Agrell points out that the number seven is often found in the Greek magical papyri in connection with operations that have erotic love as their aim (see *PGM* IV 1270ff., 1740ff.; VII 645, XII 22ff.; XXXVI 200ff.).

In the initiatory process described by the ordering of the tarok images, Gaudium expresses the stage at which the polarities expressed in the first six cards are combined or—to use the alchemical term—coagulated. This synthesis is affected through the power of love, through the power of the desire of the heart. Its completion is a joy and delight.

HAMAXA
THE CHARIOT
$H = 8$ [7]

The image of The Chariot is an archaic one among the original Mithrists. The use of sphinxes in recent embellished occult versions of the tarot is merely an Egyptomaniacal fashion statement—and a rather kitschy one at that.

In the original visual conception of The Chariot, it was perhaps a vehicle pulled by four horses and thus symbolic of the quadriga of Mithras. The myth of Mithras and his four cosmic horses is recounted in chapter 2. This is despite the fact that two horses pulling a chariot is definitely the most archaic imagery among the Indo-Europeans. These are the twin horses that pull the chariot of the Roman goddess of the dawn, Aurora. The Visconti-Sforza card even shows a female driver of the chariot—perhaps reminiscent of this image of the goddess of the dawn.

The Chariot shows the image of Mithras Triumphator—that is, Mithras (or the subject of initiation) in a triumphal march of glory after his great victory.

The vehicle itself is a symbol of the constellation(s) of the wagons or wains, also called the Bears (Ursa Major and Ursa Minor), that dominate the circumpolar night sky. The designation of these constellations with the name "wagon" or "chariot" is, by the way, very ancient among the Indo-Europeans. Homer (eighth century BCE) refers to the *hamaxa,* "chariot," constellation in the *Iliad* (XVIII, 487).

This constellation of the wagon or chariot became a symbol of the whole of the sphere of the fixed stars, the crystal heaven of the Mithrists. Remember that the eighth stoicheion of the Greek system, *theta,* is also a symbol of this level of reality.

·The Chariot·

Image by Amber Rae Broderick

Gringonneur

Visconti-Sforza

Rosenwald

The constellation of the Bear (Arktos) is mentioned prominently in the formulas of the Greek magical papyri. In (*PGM* IV.1275–1389) the constellation is called, among many other things, "the one who holds together the universe and brings to life the whole world." David Ulansey has convincingly pointed out that the astral iconography of the Tauroctony, the bull-slaying image found in most Mithraea, refers to Mithras's function as a god of the pole—or a god who has the power to shift the relationships among the causal principles that the stars represent.

The Greek word for "chariot," or "wagon," is *hamaxa,* which was borrowed into Latin and used for the same type of vehicle.

The Chariot, the vehicle of the subject of initiation, is a symbol of the crystallization of a perfected state of being in balance between motion and stasis.

IUSTITIA
JUSTICE
I = 9 [8]

The image of Justice personified as a woman holding a sword and scales is virtually universal among the cards. The image is found among the Mantegna cards bearing the title "Iustitia" (Series B 37).

The scales are emblematic of the power of Justice to weigh the relative merits of two possibilities and to determine the truth of one over the other. As portrayed in this Arcanum it is a cosmic process, not a legalistic one as we might understand it today. With the scales Iustitia determines the relative level of *ius* ("justice") of a thing. Once the determination is made, the sword is used to execute the decision.

The sword represents the power of Iustitia to decide; Latin *decidere,* "to cut (down)." The meaning of this word for the Romans was to "separate right from wrong"—or *fas* from *non-fas. Fas* means "that which is harmonious with the cosmic order." It is a force that is only opposed at the opponent's own mortal peril. Even the gods and goddesses are subject to this power.

As is usually the case in Mediterranean culture, a female form is used to represent an abstract principle.

· JUSTICE ·

Image by Amber Rae Broderick

Gringonneur

Visconti-Sforza

Mantegna

Iustitia is a late personification of the ancient abstract principle of justice. In the oldest form of Roman religious conceptions, this was encoded in the abstract principles of *ius,* "those things which are legal or just," and *fas,* "that which is in accord with cosmic order." The great Indo-Europeanist Georges Dumézil compares these concepts to the Vedic ideas of *dhaman* (or *dharman*), "(cosmic) law," and *rta* (or *vrata*), "cosmic order." In his monumental study *Archaic Roman Religion,* Dumézil comments: "*Fas* would be the mystical, invisible basis without which *ius* is not possible, and which sustains all the visible arrangements and relations defined by *ius.*"[2] Fas either exists or does not exist in a thing, time, or event—it is absolute—whereas *ius* exists in a relative and divisible way. Mundane human law is a manifestation of ius, derived from the ultimate principle of fas.

As a mythic manifestation of all this, Iustitia does not only and necessarily represent the justice of men but rather that of the whole of the cosmos. This form of absolute justice is often felt as being harsh by humans—especially by the uninitiated, for whom the necessary workings of this form of justice often seem arbitrary. The Romans also called this aspect of the force by the name of another goddess: Necessitas.

The Greek form of this goddess is Ananke, whose name means "Necessity." This is the force of compulsion in the universe that makes things be the way they are. All things—including the gods and goddesses—must bend to her will. When this was felt to be a negative force, she was often called Nemesis. She is also equated with the Greek goddess Dike ("Justice"), the daughter of Zeus and Themis ("Law"), who is one of the three Horae.

The original meaning of this Arcanum is complex and profound. It is based on an intrinsic understanding of the concept of law, both the higher law (fas) and the lower law (ius). Such law is based on the ability to separate one thing from another—the just from the unjust, based on an understanding and knowledge of the righteous and unrighteous. Here things are broken down, analyzed, and further development is made possible.

That an essentially and originally Mithraic system would be so concerned with the law is very understandable—as in his oldest Indo-European form, Mitra is the god of law, justice, and contracts of all kinds.

Structurally, Iustitia [8] and Fortuna [11] are closely related in a contrasting way. Iustitia is based on an eternally implacable and consistent force, whereas Fortuna is the essence of eternal change. Viewed from a noninitiated perspective, they may be experienced in a similar way.

In the ninth level the now crystalized and dynamic state of the subject of initiation is placed in a situation in which it is to be tested—before the court of Saturn (found in the Hermit). The ninth Arcanum brings together and harmonizes the inner and outer worlds—the laws of seven and three are dynamically harmonized in nine.

KRONOS
THE HERMIT
K = 10 [9]

On the older cards the usual image of The Hermit is that of an old man holding an hourglass through which pass the sands of time. This is clearly an attribute of the god Kronos, or Saturn, as the Romans came to call him. Kronos, of course, corresponds to the Mithraic figure of Zurvan—Eternal Time.

The representation of The Hermit holding aloft a lantern is found in the Marseilles and most later decks. This image seems to have been drawn from the classical mythological figure of Diogenes.

On at least one level this image is a symbol of old age and death—of separation from the stream of life as it is usually understood. The Hermit is always in a position high above the normal realm of life—looking down upon it. So old age and death are here not identical with our mundane experience of these things but rather are revelations concerning their true nature—or what their true nature can be if experienced from an initiated perspective.

Because Saturn is the outermost of the planetary spheres (according to ancient traditional astrology) this realm is seen as a lofty, transcendent region, far from human or terrestrial contact. It is therefore symbolized by a Hermit, and the Archon ("ruler") of that sphere is seen as such a Hermit among the planetary Archons.

· The hermit ·

Image by Amber Rae Broderick

Gringonneur

Visconti-Sforza

Lando

The metal associated with Kronos-Saturn is lead. Lead is often a symbol of death. In the Greek magical papyri, the spells intended to cause death or misfortune, and certainly to cause a person to act against their will, are often carved on lead plates, or *lamea*.[3]

Roman tradition has it that when Kronos the Titan was defeated and dethroned in Greece by his son, Zeus, the elder numen was exiled to Italy, where his reign ushered in a Golden Age. The most archaic level of Roman religion reveals that Saturn was originally the god of the sowing of seed, and his wife, Ops, was the goddess of the harvest.

The so-called SATOR square has often been associated with the influence of Saturn. It will be recalled from chapter 3 that the numerical value of the totality of this magical square equals the same number as the sum of the names of the Mithraic initiatory grades (i.e., 2,520).*

SATOR =	200 + 1 + 300 + 70 + 100	=	671
AREPO =	1 + 100 + 5 + 80 + 70	=	256
TENET =	300 + 8 + 50 + 8 + 300	=	666
OPERA =	70 + 80 + 5 + 100 + 1	=	256
ROTAS =	100 + 70 + 300 + 1 + 200	=	671
			2,520

CORAX =	3 + 70 + 100 + 1 + 60	=	234
CRYPHIUS =	3 + 100 + 10 + 80 + 5 + 10 + 6 + 200	=	414
MILES =	40 + 10 + 30 + 5 + 200	=	285
LEO =	30 + 5 + 70	=	105
MITHRA =	40 + 10 + 300 + 5 + 100 + 1	=	456
HELIODROMUS =	5+5+30+10+70+4+100+70+40+6+200	=	540
PATER =	80 + 1 + 300 + 5 + 100	=	486
			2,520

*For an outline of the complete system of esoteric number values for the Roman letters, see table 2, column 7, on page 166.

The significance of this complex mathematical symbol is that the Arcanum of Saturn-Kronos contains the sum total—in seed-form—of initiatory knowledge in the Mithraic system. Note also that the sum of the digits making up the key number 2,520 equals nine (2 + 5 + 2 = 9), which is the esoteric key number of the Saturnian sphere and the esoteric number of this Arcanum.

Nowhere in the system of the Mithraic Roman Arcana is the compilation of elements clearer than in this Arcanum—Mithraic Iranian, Greek, and Roman elements blend into a harmonious whole under the guidance of the mathematical science of the Stoics.

The original meaning of this Arcanum had to do with the separation of the essence of the initiate, or anything that is undergoing transformation, into a remote seed-form in preparation for further metamorphosis. On one level this is an Arcanum of perfection—a process brought to a completed stage.

At this stage of development, the first initiatory trials are passed before the gate to the trans-Saturnian spheres. Hereafter development of the initiate takes place within the higher spheres—in which the tests will be even more arduous than they had been in the lower ones.

LIBERA
WHEEL OF FORTUNE
L = 11 [10]

Most of the older cards show a wheellike structure upon which ride a variety of entities. The image found among the Visconti-Sforza cards shows a blindfolded female figure in the center of a wheel around which are four figures. The one at the top (who wears the ears of an ass) is labeled *regno*, "I reign"; the figure going downward on the right-hand side of the wheel is labeled *regnavi*, "I reigned"; the one at the bottom of the wheel, an old man, is labeled *sum sine regnum,* "I am without reign"; and the figure on the ascending left-hand side of the wheel is labeled *regnabo,* "I shall reign."

In subsquent versions of this Arcanum, these simple icons are replaced by strange and exotic figures of later derivation. A leonine

Image by Amber Rae Broderick

Visconti-Sforza   Court de Gebelin   Rider-Waite

figure may descend on one side, while a figure apparently meant to represent Anubis or Typhon-Set rises on the other. The Rider-Waite image is most fanciful and modern in this regard. The Court de Gebelin card (ca. 1787) shows a winged and crowned figure at the apex of the wheel with a descending figure with the tail of a lion and an ascending figure with the head of a monstrous beast. Clearly the implication is that evil and good rise and fall according to an impersonal and amoral—even chaotic—process.

The image of a female figure holding a scepter and a globe found among the Gringonneur cards is most probably the image of The World; however, many researchers have identified it as the "Wheel of Fortune" or, better said, "Fortuna."

Machiavelli, in his book *The Prince* (ch. 25), describes the Renaissance view of Fortuna as a great (and blind) natural force—such as a floodtide, which seems unstoppable. Yet, those who have heeded the dangers in time may be able to take measures against coming misfortune. Fortuna will exert her will, regardless of how people act. Only by preparing for the inevitable turn of the wheel, and by being in tune with the times, can a prince hope to overcome the compelling force of Fortuna. This view is fully illustrated in the Visconti-Sforza version of the image.

Fortuna is like a wheel that turns inevitably. What was up yesterday is bound to be down tomorrow. Fortuna is ever changing; if humans are unchanging also, they will unavoidably fall victim to Fortuna. Only those who change, who are in a process of transformation, may escape her ravages.

There is more than just a bit of chaos in this description. In contrast to the force of Iustitia, which is steadfast and constant, the force of Fortuna is fickle and totally unpredictable. Iustitia is the manifestation of a cosmic force, and Fortuna that of a chaotic one.

The old Roman name of this Arcanum was most likely Libera, who is the goddess of growth and change. In Rome she was paired with her male counterpart, Liber, the god of wine and sexual liberation. He was later equated with Bacchus-Dionysus. Both Libera and Liber were honored in the festival known as the Liberalia, held on March 17. This historical root may account for the nature of most of St. Patrick's Day celebrations.

The Arcanum of Libera refers to the eternal force of change in the universe. It is emphasized that this is a blind and impersonal force of Destiny—with no regard for morality.

The developmental process described by the tarok here enters into a chaotic stage, which opens the process to a wider number of possibilities than had previously been the case.

MAGNITUDO
STRENGTH
M = 12 [11]

The image of the Strength card in the tarot varies quite widely. Some of the older cards show a female figure breaking a stone column (as in the Gringonneur card), while the Visconti-Sforza card shows a male figure holding a club over a lion. This male image is obviously a reflection of Hercules, whose weapon of choice is a club and who, as a youth, slew the Thespian lion. (Later, as the first of his twelve labors, Hercules killed the Nemean lion without weapons.) The most familiar image is that of a female figure subduing a lion with an apparently supernatural strength. Although the images may vary, the meaning is quite clear.

In each instance the image is a demonstration of the power of the human being over lower forces, symbolized as either a part of the mineral or animal kingdoms.

The predominance of the appearance of female figures in this apparently masculine Arcanum is accounted for by the fact that abstract principles are almost always personified as female figures in classical iconography.

The original Roman name of this Arcanum was probably Magnitudo, which is a simple translation of "strength," but one that also carries the important nuance of moral virtue. Obviously the strength referred to is something more than merely physical. Magnitudo is also used as a synonym for *robur,* the oak tree, which is an enduring symbol of loyalty and virtue.

·STRENGTH·

Image by Amber Rae Broderick

| Gringonneur | Visconti-Sforza | Court de Gebelin |

Magnitudo is the power of the human mind or psyche to overcome the brute force of the animal kingdom (as expressed both within and without the human species) and to master the insensate mineral kingdom.

In his "Oration on the Dignity of Man," the Italian Renaissance philosopher Giovanni Pico della Mirandola describes a Neoplatonic view of the nature of humans as being indeterminate. Humans may be nothing more than plants if they are dominated by their appetites, or nothing more than beasts if they are governed by their senses. But if their intellects rule, they may become truly human and ultimately, if they become one with their spirits, they may become like unto gods.

This is the power of the psyche to exert rulership over randomness in the universe and to have knowledge of the factors ruled by implacable Necessity (= Arcanum 9).

Magnitudo is necessary to overcome the randomness of the Wheel of Fortune, and either to prepare the soul for the test it will encounter in the realm of Noxa, of The Hanged Man, or to avoid the realm of punishment altogether and pass on to the transformative Arcanum of Death (Orcus).

Noxa
The Hanged Man
N = 13 [12]

The image found on the Visconti-Sforza card shows a man hanging in inverted position by the left foot. His hands are behind his back—probably bound. This is clearly a depiction of some type of torture, though the figure seems serene.

On the Gringonneur card there are the added features of two money bags being held in both hands. This addition does not seem to be unique, as the Rosenwald card, dated from the early 1700s, shows the same money bags.

The implication of the money bags is that some sort of penalty or fine is being paid by the hanging man. The two money bags are symbolic of the fact that what is going on in the image involves an exchange of value. Something is being given in return for something else; a debt is being repaid.

Image by Amber Rae Broderick

Visconti-Sforza   Gringonneur   Rosenwald

Hanging of various types was widely used in ancient, medieval, and modern European societies as a form of either corporal or capital punishment—depending on how the hanging was carried out.

The more current name, "The Hanged Man," is merely a description of what is seen when one looks at the card. This is also true for many of the other cards. The older, more esoteric names for the Arcana were probably more evocative of their meanings—if they were not, in fact, trying to hide or conceal their interpretations.

For this Arcanum the evocative interpretation was probably *Noxa,* from a Latin word for the harm or pain that comes from "punishment."

Traditionally, and certainly within ancient mystery cults, punishment and suffering were often considered necessary parts of the transformative or initiatory process. This is something that has often been ignored in modern times, so intent on always having a good time. But The Hanged Man is an image of just what it appears to be—a man being tortured. He is being punished or having to atone for some misdeed. This atonement is purgative and ultimately strengthening.

If the qualities inherent in Magnitudo are strong enough, the punishment or atonement of Noxa may be unnecessary. However, the roads from both lead into the realm of Orcus—Death.

It should be noted that in the transition between the older Greek system of mysteria attached to the twenty-four stoicheia and the Arcana associated with the Roman letters, it was after this thirteenth image that the sequence was altered.

ORCUS
DEATH
O = 14 [13]

The Visconti-Sforza image of this card shows a skeletal figure holding a bow in his left hand and an arrow in his right. The bow and arrow are the favorite weapon of Mithras. The figure has a blindfold lifted from his piercing eyes. Death has been faced and overcome.

More usual are the images found on the Gringonneur and Lando cards, which show skeletal figures mowing down humans of all social and economic backgrounds with a scythe. The Gringonneur card shows the skeleton riding a horse and with the Visconti-Sforza figure shares the feature of the lifted blindfold. Fortuna (and Iustitia) may be blind—but Death has his eyes wide open.

The use of a horse in conjunction with symbols of Death goes far back into the Indo-European tradition. A horse was often considered the bearer of the dead from this world to the realm of Death. Also it is interesting to note that the Greeks often called Hekate, the goddess of the Underworld, ἵππος, "horse."

The common title of this card is Death. In the most archaic level of Italic religion the god of death and of the realm of the dead is called Orcus. This would seem to have been the title of this Arcanum among the Mithraic Romans.

Entry into the realm of Orcus is one of the critical moments in the story of development outlined in the symbolism of the tarok. Along with the Wheel of Fortuna, The Hanged Man, The Tower, and Judgment, the realm of Death indicates a quality of potential disaster and catastrophe. Tests must be passed and ordeals withstood.

Because of the extreme importance of the overcoming of death and the winning of immortality in the initiatory warrior cult of the Mithraic Romans, this Arcanum obviously has a special role to play. The self of the initiate must be prepared, through Magnitudo and/or Noxa, in order to pass into and out of the realm of Orcus. The realm of the dead is a place of transformation, but it is without doubt also a place dangerous to the soul of the initiate. It is a place where the soul can undergo a metamorphosis, or a place where it can die altogether. The preparation in the previous stages of initiation will determine which it will be. (This latter possibility is often ignored in modernistic feel-good essays on the symbolism of the tarot.)

Sigurd Agrell suggested that this Arcanum represented a Roman synthesis of the fourteenth and eighteenth Greek stoicheia (the *xi* and *sigma,* respectively). See chapter 3 for a discussion of these in their Greek

M

·ᴅᴇᴀᴛʜ·

Image by Amber Rae Broderick

Visconti-Sforza   Gringonneur   Lando

context. Part of the reason for this combination, besides the necessity to reduce the system from twenty-four to twenty-two, was perhaps the desire to preserve the sacred combination of the Stars-Moon-Sun, which seems to have had a special significance going all the way back to the Iranian root tradition.

Pluvia
Temperance
P = 15 [14]

Universally, the image of the Arcanum of Temperance is that of a female figure (seated in the Gringonneur card) who holds two vessels of water. She pours liquid from one vessel into another, mixing their contents. In the Mantegna card (Series B XXXIIII) she is doing the same—and there is a small animal (probably an ermine, a symbol of royalty) gazing at its own reflection in a small mirror.

Clearly the image refers to the idea of the necessity of the proper mixture of essential components for the success of the transformative process.

The word "temperance" comes from the Latin verb *tempero*, which means "to be moderate, to control oneself." But it can also mean "to mix properly," or "to regulate something." This reveals a deep-level meaning of the Arcanum: in this Arcanum initiates must learn to mix and regulate the various elements within their systems. Only after this level of control is attained can the initiatory realm of the Devil be entered. If this temperance is not attained, the realm of the Devil (Mithras) could spell disaster.

Temperance refers to the right (rational) mixture of elements as being the essence of a certain type of transformation.

The older Roman name of this Arcanum was likely Pluvia, "rain (water)." Symbolically, this indicated "one who drinks water rather than wine" and may also be a reference to the old Roman practice of mixing water with wine to dilute its intoxicating effects. (That this is done in the Roman Catholic ritual of the Eucharist is only a sign of its pagan Roman, and Mithraic, origin.)

·TEMPERANCE·

Image by Amber Rae Broderick

Visconti-Sforza

Gringonneur

Mantegna

Also connecting the name Pluvia to the fundamental idea of temperance as a mixing of the elements is the symbol of the phenomenon of rain. When it rains, the elements are mixed in the heavens: water is mixed with air; heaven and earth are linked with the fire of lightning. This is a powerful and extremely archaic symbolic phenomenon. The rains bring forth the fruits of the earth—the culmination of a process of growth.

The association of this Arcanum with rain is even more strongly suggested by the contents of the entire 7th chapter of the *Bundahishn,* which relates how the great deluge of rain was brought about by a mixture of the elements and how it, in turn, mixed the elements of earth, making way for the greater creation. This temperance was ruled by the star Sirius (Tishtar), which may account for the similarity in the iconography between the star and Temperance. The correlation between rain and creation, and re-creation, is found throughout Persian literature.

Emerging from the realm of Death, the initiate must exercise the feminine virtue of Temperance to continue the development of the metamorphosing self. The Devil marks the masculine side of this transformed self—Temperance is thought to represent the feminine side.

QUIRINUS
THE DEVIL
Q = 16 [15]

It seems that fewer of The Devil cards have survived from the very oldest tarot packs than any other card, which is not surprising. It is likely that people intentionally destroyed the cards, or took them out of the deck, so they could not occur in readings. The symbolism of the card remains archaic and rich, however.

Among the old cards we see two basic images of The Devil. One shows him with a bestial face (horned and winged) either sitting or standing on a pedestal with two young human figures (one light, one dark) and chained or tied to the pedestal. This is rather reminiscent of

↑

· The Devil ·

Image by Amber Rae Broderick

Lando

Visconti-Sforza
(Reconstructed)

Jean Galler
(eighteenth century)

the mental image of Zurvan-Aion in relation to his two sons—Ohrmazd (Light) and Ahriman (Darkness). In the Lando Tarot (ca. 1760) The Devil is shown with a second face on his belly, a feature also found in the Parisian Tarot of the 1600s.

The other type of image, seen on the Galler card, shows a devilish figure who is conspicuous because he has four faces: one on the front of his head, one on his chest, and two on his knees. Remarkably, the Iranian god Zurvan is called the god of four faces![4] These four faces are explained in his four forms, or hypostases: Zurvan (Eternal Time) in the center, surrounded by a triumvirate of Ashoqar (Virility), Frashoqar (Splendidness), and Zaroqar (Old Age). These exemplify the effects of Time on all things: Birth–Life–Death.

This image is universally called "The Devil," although Court de Gebelin called the card "Typhon," apparently in an attempt to make them appear more Egyptian! The designation as "the devil" must be an ancient one. It may even go back to the Avestan *daêva*, originally a word for "a god," which in orthodox Zoroastrian circles came to designate a "demon" or "devil."

In the old Roman alphabetic system, however, this Arcanum would have carried the name Quirinus. This ancient deity of war (with Mars) and peace was also the deified form of Romulus, the eponymous founder of the Eternal City. Moreover, Quirinus is sometimes identified with the god Janus—the two-faced god of beginnings and endings. In Rome the Gate of Janus was opened when the Romans were at war and closed when they were at peace. In medieval depictions of the Devil, he was often shown with two faces (one sometimes on his buttocks). Epithets of Janus include Quadriformis (= "Four-formed") and Quadrifons (= "Of four origins")—which brings us right back to the four-faced image of the seventeenth-century card!

Agrell identified the Devil with Mithras-Serapis in his aspect as the invincible god (Gk. *anikētos*, Lat. *invictus*). This identification comes primarily on numerical grounds, as the Devil and Mithras are both associated with the value sixteen.

The Devil is the intemperate masculine force juxtaposed to the feminine force of Temperance in the previous Arcanum. Having passed through the punishment and death of Arcana 13–14, the initiate has attained through the application of Temperance a quintessential state of balanced, yet dynamic (warrior-like) serenity—or *ataraxia*. The initiate has now been prepared for the even greater challenges yet to come.

Understanding of this Arcanum is provided by knowledge of, and experience in, the cycles of time and the beginning and ending of things.

Another, more Mithraic interpretation, might be that after applying Temperance to the tested and transformed self, the Human-Divine, the Anikētos/Invictus, emerges.

RUINA
THE TOWER
R = 17 [16]

All cards show the same basic symbology. There is a tower or fortification that is falling into ruins and/or is being destroyed by a bolt of lightning—which often appears to be a flame coming from the Sun rather than an electrical discharge. A common element is a crown at the apex of the tower, which is being dislodged by the force of the lightning or fire.

Although the iconography of this Arcanum is consistent, it is called by more various names than any other card. In English, French, and Italian it is named the "House of God" or the "House of the Devil"; the "Thunderbolt," "Lightning," "Fire of Heaven," or the "Arrow"; or the "Tower." This variety of names points to a certain ambivalence but also reveals an underlying consistency.

The Italian name *Il Fulmine* and the French name *Le Foudre*, both meaning "thunderbolt" or "lightning," seem archaic. They are derived from the Latin word *fulmen*, which basically means a "stroke of lightning" but which also carries the connotation of a "crushing calamity" or even an "irresistible power." Such connotations must go all the way back to the god of thunder, the Roman Jupiter, who was also called Fulgurator or Fulminator. The thunderbolts of Jupiter were his way of dealing with those whom he wished to punish.

Image by Amber Rae Broderick

Gringonneur   Visconti-Sforza   Rosenwald
                       (Reconstructed)

It is also significant that in Latin the title Fulgurator may be used to indicate a priest who interprets omens from lightning.

The name Arrow (La Sagitta or La Saetta) is also probably an ancient one. The bow and arrow is, of course, the favorite weapon of Mithras and is well represented in the iconography of the cards. It is symbolic of the sudden striking power over long distances of any divine force. This is why it is so often seen as the weapon of Eros-Cupidas (Cupid).

In all instances the interpretation of the poetic name can be inferred as "ruination." For this reason, it is thought to be most likely that the original Latin divinatory name for this Arcanum was simply *Ruina*.

Perhaps significantly, this card, along with that of The Devil, is missing from the Visconti-Sforza deck. It is likely that these cards were, for whatever reasons, the most feared or ominous of the cards and were often enough discarded from the packs to cause them to disappear from all collections of that version of the Arcana.

The original meaning of this Arcanum is clearly that of the catastrophic—and hence transformative—effects of certain forms of divine influence on works of men. Kingdoms may be destroyed in a flash. This force works like a bolt from the blue on the world of humans—unlike that of Fortuna, which acts in a regular, predictable way. Predictable, that is, if one knows the laws of Fortuna. But here are no such laws when it comes to the Fulgurator.

Agrell maintains that the meaning of this Arcanum was imported from the twenty-third stoicheion in the Greek system (*psi*), the image of which (Ψ) he relates to a trident symbol used in archaic times as an emblem of the thunderbolt of Zeus.

The Tower portrays a final purifying test that will lead either to ruin or to entry into the realm of the celestial triad of Stars-Moon-Sun. Lightning purges and purifies the initiate and is an expression of the power of a god (or a devil). But most importantly, it acts as a bridge from the Quadriform Arcanum 16 into the celestial triad so important in transformative Mithraic symbolism. This is the effect of the fire from heaven on the Quadriformis—which leads entry into the celestial triad—specifically through the Star(s).

In the supposed Greek system of the tarok it is the Arcanum of The Tower that is most dramatically removed to a new place in the sequence of images—to the twenty-third place. The significance of this is that in the Greek system there is an emphasis on the role of catastrophe, on sudden change or reversal of forces, in the transformative process. In the Greek system, it is the final test and purification coming just before the ultimate perfection of *omega*—although there, as here, there is the possibility—even probability—of utter and irreversible catastrophe.

STELLA
THE STAR
S = 18 [17]

This Arcanum can be shown with a wide variety of images. The Visconti-Sforza card is the simplest iconographically. The female figure grasps an eight-rayed star with her left hand. The theme of eightfoldedness is repeated throughout the other images.

On the D'Este image we see an image that prefigures a more common depiction connected with The Moon—two astrologers gazing at an eight-rayed star while consulting a chart. This chart seems to be inscribed with the shape of a crescent moon.

The most common image of The Star is the one derived from the Marseilles tradition. This was later used as the model for the most famous deck of all, the Rider-Waite deck. In that tradition we see a naked woman emptying two amphorae or pitchers of water—one into a stream and one onto the ground. Above her are eight stars, each of which has eight rays. It is noteworthy that seven of the stars seem to be arrayed around a central star—a configuration suggestive of the relationship of Ursa Major to the Pole Star.

The name of this Arcanum is consistently either the singular, "The Star," or more rarely the plural, "Stars" (Stellae). In the case of the singular name, the star is sometimes named as the Dog Star Sirius (called Tishtar or Tîr by the Persians). The importance of this star is enormous

·The STAR·

Image by Amber Rae Broderick

Visconti-Sforza

D'Este

Marseilles

in Persian and Egyptian lore, but it seems to have lost significance in Mithraic doctrine. It is more likely, especially given the array of the seven stars (Ursa Major) around it, that the star in question is the Pole Star.

When the plural "Stars" is indicated as the name of the Arcanum, we can associate the name with several constellations important to the Mithraic mythology. They may be the stars of the constellation Taurus. This is supported by Agrell's idea that this Arcanum occupied the fourteenth position in the Greek system, and the number fourteen is associated with the Bull in Persian mythology.

It is also possible that the constellation in question is that of Perseus (17 stars), which, according to David Ulansey's study, is identified with Mithras. This too would fit well, since starlight in general is often identified with the essence of Mithras. Remember that Mithras is said to have been born from the rock, which is the rock-crystal heaven whence the starlight first emerged.

A third possibility is that of the constellation of Ursa Major, the Great Bear, or Great Wagon, called Haptôk-ring by the Persians. This is supported by the direct evidence of the cards in the tradition of the Marseilles deck. There we see eight stars, but one is clearly larger than, and somehow different from, the other seven. There are seven stars in the Great Bear. Also the lore we have from the Hermetic magical papyri indicates that the constellation of the Bear (Arktos or Arktē) was thought to have the power to turn the pole and shift the axis of the cosmos.

The original meaning of this Arcanum is intelligence. Starlight in general is connected with Mithras as the bringer of divine intelligence to humanity. This intelligence is subsequently reflected in the Moon and is produced directly in the Sun.

Upon entry into this Arcanum, the initiate gains access to the fifth level of Mithraic initiation. Here the candidate is identified with the stars. As mentioned above, the stars in question may be the stars of the constellation Perseus (= "the Persian"), who was equated with Mithras. Thus, we have a perfect correspondence between this grade of initiation and these names—"the Persian" or "Mithras."

Here the candidate comes into possession of certain gifts of intelligence—the secret for the stars is revealed: intelligence has the power to move the stars and to create and destroy the world.

With entry into this Arcanum, the initiate has made a way into the astral or sidereal realm that will lead the initiate through a threefold process from the realm of the fixed stars to the Moon, and from there to the Sun.

As mentioned above, in the Greek system this Arcanum held the fourteenth position. In chapter 3 we noted the probability that in Mithraic secret doctrines the stars in question were identified with the constellation of the Bull (Lat. Taurus, Pers. Tôrâ), as the Persian calendar made the fourteenth day of the month holy to "the Soul of the Bull" (Av. Gôshûrvan).

TRINA
THE MOON
T = 19 [18]

The iconography of The Moon card is extremely varied. The Visconti-Sforza card merely shows a female figure holding aloft a crescent moon in her right hand and a broken bow in her left. Some have speculated with good reason that this originally represented the goddess Diana. A radical departure from this image is seen in the Gringonneur card. There we see two astrologers using a book and compass to make some precise measurement of the Moon, which looms crescent-shaped overhead. Finally, the Court de Gebelin image along with the Marseilles card show the most familiar, and most mysterious, iconography. On that card we see looming between two towers a moon that seems to drip drops of blood. These drops, which are nineteen in number, are lapped at by two canines—probably both dogs. In the foreground a crayfish is seen submerged in water.

This image was subsequently used in the composition of the well-known Rider-Waite deck. This triformal image, cast between two poles (the towers), refers to the astral phenomena of the constellation of Canis (the Dog), and perhaps Scorpio, while the towers represent the

· THE MOON ·

Image by Amber Rae Broderick

| Visconti-Sforza | Gringonneur | Court de Gebelin |

two terrestrial poles of the elliptic. The key to the full understanding of this image is contained in David Ulansey's study of Mithraic astronomy, *The Origins of the Mithraic Mysteries*.

Several early commentators on the tarot, including Éliphas Lévi, note that some of the older cards differentiate between the two canine figures and that one may be construed as a wolf rather than a dog. In this case, if the image goes back to some archaic model, it is likely that the dog represents the benevolent, helpful aspect of the canine spirit, while the wolf represents that which is warlike and bellicose. The dog is the most holy animal in the Zoroastrian faith, and it was his faithful dog who helped Mithras hunt the Bull.

The name of this Arcanum refers to the chief symbol of two threefold goddesses of classical antiquity—Hekate and Selene—as well as the triple goddess of the ancient Iranians, Anahita. The fact that all of these goddesses are seen as essentially threefold gave rise to code names, or esoteric names, for this Arcanum that refer to this numerical quality. These names must have included Triformis, Trigemina, Trivia, and Trina.

This threefold aspect may be reflected in the iconography of the three creatures in the Marseilles-derived image: the wolf refers to the aspect of birth, the dog to that of life, and the crab or crayfish (derived from the image for the scorpion) to that of death.

Refer back to the iconography of the Tauroctony and you will see just how much of the symbolism of the tarok is contained in it. There the Moon and Sun loom over the scene; the constellations of many Stars are represented. A dog laps at the blood of the (lunar) Bull, whose seed is purified by the Moon to provide the Earth with all beneficial plants and herbs.

At this phase, the intelligence of the Stars is reflected in and by the Moon. This is what leads to wisdom: thoughtful reflection on the contents of the mind. Remember that the ancient Mithrists (as well as the Indo-Europeans in general) used honey as a symbol of wisdom and held that it was derived from the Moon.

The nineteen drops appear to be a signature indicating the true position of the image in the sequence.

After passing through the sphere of the Moon, the candidate for initiation is ready to become a Courier of the Sun.

VICTOR-UNUS
THE SUN
V = 20 [19]

The iconography of this Arcanum is rather diverse. On the Visconti-Sforza card we see the personified Sun being born aloft by a cherubic winged figure, while on the Gringonneur card we find a female figure on the ground beneath the Sun. She is spinning wool. On the Marseilles card—from which most modern decks are derived—we see two cherubic figures flanking the Sun overhead. The Sun is dripping thirteen varicolored drops—reminiscent of the drops falling from the Moon in the previous Arcanum.

The original image was most likely that of the Sun, Helios (Ἥλιος), flanked by the two Mithraic torchbearing twins, Cautes and Cautopates.

The Sun is important in most systems of religion and magic. Because of the established importance of the specific constellation of the Stars-Moon-Sun in Mithraic mysticism, we may look to that system for more insight into the meaning of the Sun in the tarok.

Among the Mithrists this Arcanum would have been principally associated with Sol Invictus—the "Invincible Sun." Therefore its title or name would have been Victor. This reverberates with the Arcanum of the Devil (Quirinus), who is also called the Invincible (Anektos or Invictus). Here the close relationship between—but not identity of—Mithras and Helios is shown. Mithras is the Devil, Helios is the Sun.

The Sun is often invoked in operations aimed at gaining victory or success in the Hermetic Greek magical papyri (e.g., *PGM* VII.1020, XII.271ff., XIII.340ff., and XXXVI.213ff.).

The essence of the difference between the two is revealed by the numerical symbolism attached to each Arcanum. The Sun is also called Unus ("the One") and hence carries the title Uniformis, the "Single-formed." The esoteric number of the Arcanum is $19 = 1 + 9 = 10 = 1 + 0 = 1$.

· THE SUN ·

Image by Amber Rae Broderick

Visconti-Sforza

Gringonneur

Marseilles

This is contrasted with the titles of the Devil (Quadriformis, the "Four-formed") and the Moon (Triformis, the "Three-formed").

The Sun is the unification and synthesis of all the development that has taken place through the Arcana. This is the light of the stars focused into a singular point and guided by proper measurement and reflection (The Moon).

This leads to success and victory in all things.

It is in the realm of the Sun that the seed of the primal man, Gâyomart, is purified—and from this humanity has its heritage and destiny (see *Bundahishn,* ch. XV.1).

In the Sun the sidereal triad is completed—and the initiate is prepared for the final Judgment. The possibility of utter catastrophe still remains. The process of circulation through the triad of the Stars-Moon-Sun is clearly prefigured in the precession of Gôshûrvan ("the soul of the ox") described in the *Bundahishn,* ch. IV.4.

XIPHIAS
JUDGMENT
X = 21 [20]

The iconography of the image of this Arcanum is fairly consistent throughout the older cards. On the Visconti-Sforza card we see the scene of the resurrection of bodies from a tomb presided over by a male figure similar to the one found on the Hierophant or Pope card. Two angelic beings blow long trumpets. The Gringonneur card has only the two angelic figures with their trumpets, and there is the indication of some sort of meteorological phenomenon radiating from the clouds above the tombs. On the Marseilles card there is but one angel with a trumpet. Both the Marseilles and Visconti-Sforza cards have three figures being resurrected, while the Gringonneur card shows seven.

It is likely that in the original Iranian vision of this icon there were not angels, but fravashis, calling the dead across the Chinvat Bridge to the other world. It is interesting to note that the idea of a physical resurrection, later to become so important in Judaism and primitive Christianity, was originally an Iranian innovation.[5]

·JUDGMENT·

Image by Amber Rae Broderick

Visconti-Sforza

Gringonneur

Marseilles

The importance of the Chinvat Bridge, as described in the *Bundahishn* (ch. XII.7), can be favorably compared to that of the Bifröst Bridge in the Germanic tradition.

The fravashis are the original souls of the good spiritual creation, which eventually find their way to incarnation as human beings. They are souls that have *chosen* the Good by their own free will and so are the great cosmic warriors of Ohrmazd. These keep a record of the deeds of individuals, and when they die the fravashi judges the dead: the good cross the bridge to Paradise; the wicked fall into an infernal region, back into incarnation. In this form the fravashi is a manifestation of the goddess Daêna, "True Religion," whom we saw invoked in the description of the final stoicheion of the Greek system: *omega*.

It is also likely that the original image contained the shape of a comet. Such comets were seen as signs of final judgment in ancient times among the Iranians as well as other peoples. In ancient Iranian astrology the planets were less important than the fixed stars, and predictions were often made by observing the appearances of unpredictable phenomena—such as novae, comets, and the like—in certain segments of the night sky. These observations were made by trained priests who tended the sacred fires in night vigils on mountaintops in remote regions.

In later (Christianized) versions of the iconography, the comet is replaced by angel with a trumpet. This is an iconographical representation of the text found in Matthew 24:31: "And [the Son of man] shall send his angels with a great sound of a trumpet, and they shall gather together his elect from the four winds, from one end of heaven to the other." The Greek word used for "trumpet" here is σαλπιγξ (*salpinx*), "war trumpet," which is what the ancient astronomer Ptolemy called a certain kind of comet.

The old Greek, and eventually Latin, code name of this Arcanum was probably Xiphias. This literally means "sword" or "sword star" and refers to a comet. Comets were thought to be signs of judgments from the gods—and in this particular instance Xiphias was considered to be a sign sent forth by the god Mars as a foreboding catastrophe from above. Thus, the poetic code name Xiphias is a symbol of the abstract quality, Judgment.

This is the Arcanum of the final sundering of ignorance from enlightenment, the mortal from the immortal, the initiate from the noninitiate.

When considering the eschatology of the Mithrists and their possible doctrine of the resurrection of bodies, Cumont paraphrases chapter 30 of the *Bundahishn* in his *Mysteries of Mithras:* "All will sally forth from the tombs, will assume their former appearance, and recognize one another. Humanity entire will unite in one grand assembly, and the god of truth will separate the good from the bad."[6]

The idea of the final test before the final transformation into a living divinity took place was taken by Ruina, or The Tower or Psolos in the older Greek system—but here the catastrophic aspect of Judgment is invoked.

ZODIACUS
THE WORLD
Z = 22 [21]

Some older images of The World may show a youthful masculine figure in the midst of the zodiacal signs. This is the third man of the original Roman triumvirate, or three men, which become the trumps.

However, it seems that the predominant image is that of a female.

In the case of the male figure, it is a reflection of the cosmic man, the Ymir of the Norse, the Yama of the Vedic Aryans, the Gâyomart of the Avestan Iranians, the Anthrōpos (or Logos) of the Hermetic and Neoplatonic Greeks, and the Adam Kadmon of the Hebrews.

But the female image is perhaps more powerful from an initiatory perspective. This is because the female aspect is thought to be the third component of the soul emblematic of the end of the initiatory journey. The ancient Iranians, like the ancient Germanics, held that warriors had attendant spirits in female shape who met them upon death. Among the Norse these were known as *valkýrjur,* and among the Iranians as *fravashis.*

·The WORLD·

Image by Amber Rae Broderick

Gringonneur   Visconti-Sforza   Marseilles

On the Marseilles card we see the female figure surrounded by the four heavenly beasts of the zodiac—the Bull, the Lion, the Eagle, and the Man. These are representative of the entire zodiac, as they are the four so-called fixed signs of the four elements: earth, fire, water, and air, respectively.

The image of the female figure holding a globe and wand, as seen on the Gringonneur card, has been traced back to that of Persephone-Proserpina—who is given a pomegranate and scepter by Pluto to rule over fertility and luck.

As evocative of the final state of initiation as the image might be, the name of the Arcanum is even more telling. Among the older cards, the name "The World" or "The Universe," which is the real meaning of the term *world*, is practically the only one we find. The literal translation into Latin would, of course, be *Mundus*. However, the Marseilles card and the circle or ring in the Gringonneur card point the way to the secret code name: Zodiacus. The zodiac contains all living creatures and forms the barrier between the inner realm of the planets and the outer realm of the fixed stars. When the initiate has permanently reached the sphere of the zodiac, initiation is complete, and that initiate is beyond the influence for the stars—having become a part of them himself.

The World defines the last stage of initiation. This is marked by an identification in form and nature—if not a complete merger or unification—between the personal or subjective universe and the greater objective universe. The initiatory process is complete, and the initiate has reached a stage of development wherein immortality is gained and mastery over Destiny is achieved.

MEANING OF THE ROMAN SYSTEM

When viewed as a whole, the Roman system of Arcana illustrates a process of initiation as well as a cosmological map of the workings of the world. Originally, this system existed in a pagan, pre-Christian context—most probably that of the Mithrists of the late Imperial period.

The original function of the system was to give a kind of mnemonic index to the processes of the world and initiatory development in the world. Already in Greek times these had probably been keyed to divinatory meanings—if this was the code of the world, a code that stemmed from the gods and goddesses and that they could therefore understand, then this system also provided a means for communication between the divinities and humanity.

When viewed and experienced as a whole, the system is profound in its ability to enlighten the Fool, the initiate, in that Fool's journey through life and through the world.

The Fool, like the Bull (Apis), enters into the world of initiation without preconceived notions—but open to anything. Through the practice of magic, the Bacatus is able to make his way into the world of the divinities—first experiencing the heavenly goddess (Caeles), then the goddess of the elements (Diana), and finally the god of the cycles (Eon). After this experience the initiate has become a Priest (Flamen) and applies the arts of the latter to his understanding. With these arts the gates to ecstasy (Gaudium) are opened and the initiate mounts the heavenly vehicle of the Chariot (Hamaxa) to begin the first of a series of tests.

Initially, he must pass through the gate of Justice (Iustitia), which will prove whether he has been rightly transformed in his experience to this point. Next, he is separated from the world as a Hermit in the realm of Kronos. Upon emerging from this stage, he has attained to the higher grades of the secret priesthood.

This is only the beginning of a new series of tests, however. In this liberated state the initiate is cast into the chaotic realm that is the Wheel of Fortuna, ruled by the ancient goddess Libera. To overcome this chaotic force successfully, the initiate must apply sufficient Strength (Magnitudo), or be subjected to purifying Punishment (Noxa), to enter into a realm of transfiguration—that of the subterranean Orcus (Death).

Only if the elements of his being can be made to undergo proper Temperance—that is, mixture—in the realm of Pluvia, will the initiate be able to beneficially enter into the sphere of Quirinus (the Quadriformis), or Devil, who corresponds to Mithras. At this point the initiate will have reached the first stage of perfection. But the transformations are not at an end—if he dares to go on.

If further steps toward final perfection, or deification, are taken, the candidate must be subject to the thunderbolt that will bring all that is not essential to ruin (Ruina). If there is anything left, it will be the perfect seed that can rise to the Stars (Stellae) and receive their intelligence. From there it will cycle in a threefold process from the Stars to the Moon (Trina) and finally to the Sun (Unus), where the seed-form separated after the electric ruination process is focused and made a unified whole.

But even this focused form must be put to the final test and the final transformation. It is judged by the being of the absolute under the sign of Xiphias—the sign of Judgment. After this the initiate, now having become as one of the immortal stars, enters the realm of Zodiacus with mastery over the force of Destiny.

It might be wondered at this juncture as to how such initiatory images could have been made a part of a divinatory system. Because the images were keyed to the letters of an alphabet—first Greek and then Roman—the attachment of the images to an oracular system of sortilege was natural and expected. But beyond that, the initiatory icons themselves have a divinatory dimension because the unfoldment of life is not a continuous, linear process. Elements of the life process can be existent and influential in the story of an individual at any point in time (Zurvan). Divination focuses the attention of the individual on these elements on a continuous basis, if used correctly and with reverence.

It must be emphasized again that this process is a description of something that came at the end of a long historical development— one that may have had its origins in Iran, developed further in the Middle East, and matured among the Greek Stoics of Tarsus, before reaching a decadent stage among the Roman soldiers of the late empire.

THE GYPSIES AND THE ROMAN SYSTEM

Before leaving the topic of the Roman system and the tarot, it is interesting to note that the long-assumed link between the tarot and the Romani people (Gypsies) is confirmed, but not as is usually thought. Neither the Romani people nor the tarot images have their origins in Egypt, but both do have their origins in another common locale: central Asia. Both the tarot images and the Romani people seem to have migrated along similar paths, at roughly the same time near the end of the European Middle Ages. It is surely no fluke that the Romani folk and the tarot images appear in Europe at virtually the same time. It cannot be proved that the Romani people used the images at this early time or actually brought them into Europe—nor is this likely. What is more likely is that the Romani followed a parallel path of migration with the images, and that when the images surfaced in Europe, the Romani perhaps took them up in a spirit of immediate recognition of long lost friends.

THE ROLE OF THE EGYPTIAN TRADITION

Throughout this book references are made to symbols and divinities of the ancient Egyptians. This is especially true in appendix C on the so-called magical disk of Pergamon. At least beginning with the Greeks, the Western world has had an ongoing fascination with Egypt. The Romans continued this feeling and added to it. It must be said that many classical authors idealized Egypt, while others scorned and mocked it. Agrell consistently referred back to symbols of Egypt at every stage of his investigation but refrained from trying to link the tarok system to the twenty-four consonantal signs of the hieroglyphic scheme. The traditions of Khem—or their imagined traditions—have been the fodder of New Age thinkers for well over two thousand years. The great Egyptologist Erik Hornung outlines the history of this phenomenon in his book *The Secret Lore of Egypt: Its Impact on the West* (Cornell University Press, 2001).

Agrell was of the opinion that the alphabetic/numerological system that underlies the tarok was of Near Eastern and not Egyptian origin, because no Egyptian system of thought seems to correspond to the underlying scheme in the way that Greek, Roman, Semitic, and especially Persian material does.[7] However, in the case of the magical disk of Pergamon, he made heavy use of Egyptian hieroglyphics to explain the fields of the disk.

Because we now know that there was a Persian cult of Mithra practiced at the capital of Persepolis as early as 400 BCE, it appears that contact between Mithrists and the Egyptian culture could have taken place after the conquest of Egypt by the Persians in 525 BCE. Darius I would have had many of these Mithra-cult followers in his company in Egypt. This too could have been the origin of the connection that ultimately results in the famous "Mithras liturgy" spell found in the Greek magical papyri (*PGM* IV.475–834), which of course actually stems from Egyptian soil. Erik Hornung notes that Thoth is first referred to as the "thrice greatest" at the time when the Persian emperor Darius I was also the pharaoh of Egypt. He also reminds us that the Egyptian language has no superlative degree, as do Indo-European languages, so this Egyptian formula may have been a way to indicate the "Greatest Thoth of All." Was this formula created in conjunction with an interplay with Persian ideas?

It would be very seductive to attempt to place a great deal of importance on the twenty-four consonantal signs of ancient Egyptian hieroglyphics, but we must remember that this system is really a reconstruction by modern Egyptologists and has no documented codified existence in the ancient record. The names of these signs too are modern, often very well-informed, attributions. However, the intention of the present work is to open new questions as much as it is to give final answers, so this too may be a field of future inquiry for some enterprising esotericist.

A NOTE ON THE HEBREW SYSTEM

What has just been outlined here, of course, seems to call into question many modern occult speculations, or traditions, surrounding the tarot and its supposed original connections with the Hebrew Kabbalah. But what this information may actually be able to do is open a new door on the connection between the Kabbalah and the tarot. There could have been either an independent adaptation of the Mithraic lore or an adaptation of the Hellenistic synthesis (such as we find in with the Kabbalistic cosmology). In this case, practitioners of the Hebrew tradition would have been responsible for their own reduction of the images from twenty-four to twenty-two. It is also possible that the key to the imagery is based on the Aramaic system of letters employed by the Mithrists in Asia Minor. Aramaic is a Semitic language closely related to Hebrew and the common language of the Jews living in the Middle East. It was also used as the administrative language of the Persian Empire as early as the days of Cyrus the Great. It too made use of the twenty-two letters commonly used by most Semitic languages of the time.

It is worth emphasizing that the connections between the Jews and Persians are deep and firmly rooted in esoteric dimensions. Beginning from the time of Cyrus the Great (ca. 550 BCE) forward, there was a vigorous and vital cultural presence of the Jews in the Persian Empire. The majority of the Hebrew Bible was composed during the time when Judea was actually a province of the Achaemenid Empire and many Persian ideas entered the Jewish religion at that time and after. Politically, militarily, and culturally the Jews were important allies of the Persian emperors. With periods of brief exceptions, the Jews enjoyed a close relationship with Iran until the anomalous revolution of 1979. It is noteworthy that the Hebrew word for "mystery," in the sense of a profound esoteric *mysterion,* not just a secret hidden from prying eyes, is *râz.* This is a Persian word borrowed into Hebrew, and biblically it only appears in the Book of Daniel. The word is found in Jewish magical literature such as in the manual known as the *Sefer ha-Razim,* "The Book of Mysteries." The Kabbalah itself, should its roots go back to the last few centuries BCE, would be based on Iranian doctrines of divine and cosmological emanations. This was noted by one of the earliest secular scholars of the Kabbalah, Adolphe Franck, in 1843. Gershom Scholem's careful research showed that Kabbalistic literature had its origins from the second to thirteenth century, both in the Middle East and later in Spain. Certainly some oral traditions could have been considerably older.

As the application of Hebrew letters to the tarot has been shown to be a modern innovation, the alternative view is that the deepest esoteric connection would most likely be to the Roman system of twenty-two letters. In any event, a new door to understanding not only the tarot but also the lore informing the Kabbalah could be opened for those willing to step through it.

CONCLUSION

This whole study, first sparked by reading scholarly works by the early twentieth-century Swedish academic Sigurd Agrell, is only the intermediate stage in what could become a new and revolutionary view of the history and meaning of the tarot. Since the time of Agrell's initial publications in the 1920s and 1930s, there have been significant advances in the fields of Mithraic studies, as well as in the general esoteric field, which allow us to advance his theories beyond their original expression. One of the most important implications for the history and meaning of this symbol system is the reorientation of the system in an essentially pagan, pre- and non-Christian direction.

At the same time that the Greek and Mithraic roots of tarot symbolism are revealed, an uncanny link with the runic symbolism of the ancient Germanic peoples is also discovered. For example, by comparing the interpretations of the twenty-four chambers of the magical disk of Pergamon with the meanings of the twenty-four runes of the Older Fuþark, some amazing correspondences can be found.

It is noteworthy that the Roman system of twenty-two Arcana preserves the order of the first half of the Greek system (stoicheia 1–13) but departs from it thereafter. One of the chief significances of this study is the possibility of discovering another story in the sequence of the Arcana. Instead of following a final sequence of Death, Temperance, The Devil,

The Tower, The Star, The Moon, The Sun, Judgment, and The World, we discover an alternate sequence: The Star, The Sun, The Devil, The Moon, Death, The World, Temperance, Judgment, [Possessions?], The Tower, and [Riches?].

The Greek system provides an alternate sequence of development from that of the Roman (or Hebrew) sequence. In the Greek sequence we see that the initiate passes from the Wheel-Strength-Hanged Man—crisis point, not into Death, but to The Star (or Stars). No doubt this was a reference to some special star (perhaps the Pole Star) or constellation (perhaps Ursa Major or Perseus). From that astral level of existence, the initiate passes directly to the star of our solar system (The Sun), and from there cycles back to terrestrial existence through The Devil (associated in the Greek system with Mithras himself). Notice here that The Sun and The Devil (Helios and Mithras) are paired in the system, as they are paired in the mythology of the Mithraic Mysteries. The next cycle of three mysteria carries the initiate from the renewal of vital forces in the realm of The Moon to the experience of Death, which transfigures the candidate into the image of The World. This transformed state is then remixed in Temperance and subjected to Judgment. If the Judgment is favorable, the initiate receives a certain set of Possessions (spiritual gifts) that are then subjected to the experience of the thunderbolt (or Tower)—if the tempered and judged elements have been properly transformed, the Riches of the Kingdom will become those of the initiate. The treasure house will have been opened and entered—immortality and wisdom gained for all eternity.

It seems likely that the Greek system was not as entirely Mithraic as the Roman system became. The Greek system appears to have been much more Hermetic and Gnostic in character. In any and all cases, the findings of this book have much to tell the postmodern tarot investigator, who is now encouraged to think beyond medieval and modern restrictions and to discover even more ancient connections.

Of course, the implications for the underlying meanings of the Arcana as adapted by the Romans could be revolutionary. New relationships between and among the Arcana are revealed, and new attributes discovered.

These are perhaps best reviewed in table 1 in appendix E (see page 162).

The idea that there may be two missing Major Arcana is one of the most important considerations for serious esoteric tarok/tarot studies. Research presented in this book may give some indication of the nature and meaning of these missing Arcana. Most likely they refer to the two most magically powerful secrets, mysteries, or Arcana that the system has to teach. They would be keyed to the Greek letters *chi* and *omega*, respectively. My own insight tells me that the esoteric names of these stoicheia would have been *charis,* "gift," and *ōnos,* "price." Charis, the divine gift, is the power necessary to overcome the final test of the lightning bolt of The Tower, and ōnos is the final reward of perfection of form as a true independent attribute of the initiate.

This whole study is only the beginning of what could be a new and revolutionary phase of the understanding of the symbolism of what was, and can again be, the Magian Tarok.

Images by Amber Rae Broderick

The Persian System of Calendrical Yazatas

In the ancient Zoroastrian Persian system of theology and calendrical arrangement, the year consisted of a system of twelve approximately thirty-day months. This thirty-termed system, a sequence of thirty mythic images with a particular arrangement, is also the basis of priestly initiation—of the shaping of the *magavan,* or Magian. My book *Original Magic* (Inner Traditions, 2017) contains an initiatory curriculum based on this system. For our purposes here it is important and useful to focus on the basic iconic images invoked by the thirty yazatas as a key to the possible ultimate model for the tarok—that is, for the original model upon which the system might have been based.

The calendar was already an established system in the time of the Achaemenid Empire (550–330 BCE) and continues to be used to this day by all practicing Zoroastrians and Mazdans. It would have been the normal calendar used by the Persian Mithrists, from whom the Greeks and Romans learned the system that became what we today understand as Mithraism. It will be noted that the month was not divided into weeks in the same exact way we are used to doing, but the prototype of the weeks was present as the thirty days were divided into four sections by the insertion of the high-god, Ahura Mazda, at the beginning and three more times throughout the thirty-day cycle.

Each of the yazatas is ascribed to one of the thirty degrees in an astrological house, and all twelve constitute a ring of 360 degrees.

This system and ordering of divinities and days is known to have already been in use around 500 BCE, and thus it would have been the applicable system of images at the time when the cult of Mithra was being practiced in Persepolis. This system may then have been brought to the West in the lore of Roman Mithraism.

It is not the purpose of this book to explore the possible alternative ordering of iconic images suggested by the Avestan-Persian calendar of 2,500 years ago, but this chart of the names and symbolic meanings of the gods and goddesses, or yazatas, can be seen to be highly suggestive of what might have been the ultimate prototype of the system. Or, alternatively, it provides a new key to the mysteries of Mithra and the other yazatas of the Iranian world.

Number	Name	Translation	Interpretive Meaning
1	Ahura Mazda	Lord-Wisdom	Consciousness
2	Vohu Manah	Good Mind	Mind
3	Asha Vahishta	Best Order/ Truth	Order/Truth
4	Khshathra Vairya	Sovereign Kingdom	Sovereignty
5	Spenta Armaiti	Bounteous Devotion	Loyalty
6	Haurvatât	Perfection	Completion
7	Ameretât	Immortality	Undyingness
8	Ahura Mazda	Lord-Wisdom	Origin of Inspiration
9	Âtar	Fire	Inspiration
10	Ap	Water	Generative Force
11	Hvar	Sun	Radiance
12	Mâh	Moon	Preservation
13	Tishtrya	Star (= Sirius)	Liberation
14	Geush urvan	Bovine-soul	Vital Existence
15	Ahura Mazda	Lord-Wisdom	Origin of Mediation

Number	Name	Translation	Interpretive Meaning
16	Mithra	Contract	Mediator
17	Sraosha	Obedience	Traditional Formality
18	Rashnu	Veracity	Judgment
19	Fravashi	Immortal Soul	Individual Beings
20	Verethraghna	Victory	Breaker of Resistance
21	Vayu	Peace	Discernment of Opposites
22	Vâta	Wind	Atmosphere
23	Ahura Mazda	Lord-Wisdom	Origin of Insight
24	Daêna	Insight	True Religion
25	Ashi	Faithfulness	Rewards
26	Arshtât	Truthfulness	Justice
27	Asman	Sky (Heavenly Stone)	Origin (First Creation)
28	Zam	Earth	Manifestation
29	Manthra Spenta	Holy Word	Effective Word
30	Anaghra Raocah	Endless Light	Final and Original Perfection

A GREEK
ALPHABETIC
ORACLE

Although oracles based on the Greek and Roman letters are known to have been used in the ancient world, actual texts on how this oracular process was effected are rare. One of the clearest examples ever found is that of the so-called Oracle of Olympus. This oracle, along with other closely related inscriptions, was published by Franz Heinevetter in his 1912 dissertation *Würfel- und Buchstabenorakel in Griechenland und Kleinasien* (Dice and Letter Oracles in Greece and Asia Minor) and is treated in a practical manner in John Opsopaus's book *The Oracles of Apollo* (Llewellyn, 2017).

Due to the fact that the word order in ancient Greek was very flexible, almost any word could be made to come at the head of the oracular statement. In the translation, the word that actually heads the line is noted in Greek to show its initial letter as the key letter and word of the oracle. The translation of that initial word appears in italics and the Greek original (which follows the transcription of Heinevetter) is given in square brackets.[1] Clearly this was an oracular tool used by priests at a cult site where the oracle was delivered to the faithful who likely donated to the oracle in exchange for its wisdom. The oracle provides many different kinds of advice, telling the querent or inquirer to keep up the good work, work harder, stop what you are doing, stay longer and ask again, and so on.

From the manner in which the oracular statements are composed, it is clear that it is intended for the querent to believe that the information is being delivered by the god Apollo himself, with the diviner or oracle acting as a mere conduit for the god's advice. Little is known from ancient times about how this oracle was delivered, but it is most likely that it was a matter of great circumstance and ritual, which would impress the querent accordingly.

Several times in the text, the activity of the oracle is referred to with the Greek word χρησμος (*krēsmos*), "the answer of an oracle." Oracular answers are typically enigmatic and can be taken several different ways. The statement provided to the querent was certainly something designed to be pondered long and hard before its truth in relation to the querent's concerns were understood.

Each of the oracular statements could be the subject of long discourses by qualified classicists. It may be found that concepts embedded in the lore attached to the Greek letters in this text have some bearing on the meaning of the stoicheia that may have given rise to the images of the Magian Tarok.

A *All things* [Gk. Ἄπαντα] you will do successfully, the god [Apollo] says.

B An *assistant* [Gk. Βοηθὸν], the Pythian [= Apollo], you will have with the aid of Tyche (Fortune).

Γ *Gaia* [Gk. Γῆ = Earth] will give you the ripe fruit of your labors.

Δ *Power* [Gk. Δύναμις], ill-timed, is customarily weak.

E You *desire* [Gk. Ἐρᾷς] to see the products of suitable marriages.

Z Avoid the *surging sea* [Gk. Ζάλην] or you will be damaged.

H Bright *Helios* [Gk. Ἥλιος] sees you [Gk. Νε], and sees everything.

Θ You have helping *gods* [Gk. Θεοὺς] on this way.

I *Sweat* [Gk. Ἱδρῶτές] is present, it is better than anything else.

K Fighting with the *waves* [Gk. Κύμασι] is difficult; endure it, my friend.

Λ Passing on the *left side* [Gk. Λαιὸς] signifies everything is beautiful.

M *To work hard* [Gk. Μοχθεῖν] is necessary, but the result will be beautiful.

N A strife-bearing [Gk. Νεικηφόρον] gift concludes the oracle.

Ξ From *dry* [Gk. Ξηρῶν] shoots there is no fruit to take.

O *No* [Gk. Οὐκ] crops can be reaped that were not sown.

Π *Many* [Gk. Πολλοὺς] contests completed, the crown will be seized.

P You will proceed more *easily* [Gk. Ῥᾷον] if you stand fast for a while.

Σ *Plainly* [Gk. Σαφῶς] does Phoibos [= Apollo] speak: "Stay, friend."

T *The* [Gk. Τῶν] companions around you now will part ways with you.

Υ A high-born *undertaking* [Gk. Ὑπόσχεσιν] is held by the situation.

Φ *Carelessly* [Gk. Φαύλως] having done something, you will thereafter fault the gods.

X Succeeding you will fulfill a *golden* [Gk. Χρυσοῦν] oracle, friend.

Ψ You have this genuine *decree* [Gk. Ψῆφον] from the gods.

Ω You will have an *untimely* [Gk. Ὠμὴν] harvest, not useful.

THE MAGIC DISK
OF PERGAMON

O ne of the most important pieces of hard evidence for the divinatory uses of the Greek stoicheia, as well as their secondary connection with Egyptian lore, is found on a fascinating object uncovered
in the ruins of the ancient Greek city of Pergamon on the coast of what
is today Turkey. Archaeologists discovered a curious brazen divinatory
device there toward the end of the nineteenth century. Part of this is a
disk inscribed with a system of mysterious characters. These characters
fall into thirty-one fields, or zones. Twenty-four of these are rectangular
and are arranged in three concentric circles, and seven in the center are
triangular.

According to Sigurd Agrell, the first symbol or character in the
zone is a clue to the key term (in the Greek language) that unlocks the
secret of the zone. It is the name which functions much like the titles
of the Major Arcana in the tarot, and the sequence of which is that of
the Greek stoicheia. The first zone is to be read in a clockwise direction.

This first zone of the Pergamon disk was analyzed by Agrell as bearing a symbol for a wheel, a stylized version of the Egyptian hieroglyph
meaning "way," and an egg. Its significance is that of the beginning of a
process of growth. Agrell ascribed to it the name Abrasax.

The second zone of the disk has a symbol of a fish (in Egyptian
lore a Typhonian animal) and the Greek letter "T" (also for "Typhon").
Agrell gave this zone the name Bebon, which is a byname for Set-
Typhon found in the magical tradition.

The Magical Disk of Pergamon

A Greek *gamma* (Γ) appears to be the first sign in the third zone, the second sign is a version of the Egyptian hieroglyphic symbol for a roll of papyrus (signifying abstract idea), while the third is identified by Agrell as a flail or whip (signifying punishment or discipline). The keyword is *gnōsis,* "knowledge."

The fourth zone is headed by an equilateral cross (signifying earth), while the other three signs signify fire, water, and air, respectively. The keyword is the name of the goddess Demeter, who rules the elemental world.

The symbol heading the fifth zone is analyzed by Agrell to be a stylized version of an Egyptian hieroglyphic of two lion heads, over which is placed the disk of the sun. This is related to the lion-headed image of the god Aion in Mithraic iconography. According to Agrell the keyword is the mysterious formula Edsên (EDSHN). This is a magical formulaic word derived from Egyptian and which relates to the image of a double-headed lion.

Field number six is begun with a stylized version of the Egyptian hieroglyph for "treasure house," where sacrifices are stored. The other symbol is that of an empty hand, meaning "you need not sacrifice," according to Agrell. The keyword is conjectured to be Zemia, "monetary penalty." If this zone were indicated in a divinatory reading, it was tantamount to a demand for a sacrifice to atone for some condition in one's life.

The seventh zone begins with the sign of an empty outstretched hand. This is emblematic of friendship, according to Agrell. The second sign is thought to be that of a belt—symbol of Isis. The keyword is Hedonē, "pleasure."

The last field of the outer ring is the eighth. The first of its three signs is a ship, the second is a horn, and the third is a series of serpentine forms. The ship is a reference to the keyword of the field: Thalassa, "the sea." The serpentine forms refer to the sign of the Agathodaimōn (the good daimōn), which is often depicted as a great lion- or hawk-headed serpent in the middle of the sea in imitation of the shape of the Greek letter *thēta* (Θ).

The second circle reads in reverse order of the first—in counterclockwise direction. This reversal of order is common in Greek (and runic) inscriptions and is called boustrophedon in Greek.

The first zone of the second circle is filled with four eight-spoked wheels or stars. These are identified by Agrell as signs of the goddess Ananke, whose name means "Necessity," and her three daughters Lachesis ("Destiny"), Chlotho ("Spinner"), and Atropos ("Unchangeable"). These were known as the Fates (Gk. *Moirai*). The keyword is the name of the goddess Isis (in her aspect of Isis-Nemesis).

The tenth field contains the sickle of Kronos, the threefold sign of Hekate (the three-formed goddess of the Moon) and an Egyptian sign indicating the "realm of the dead." The keyword is Kronos.

Zone eleven contains a symbol for water, the Greek letter "B" and an Egyptian hieroglyph depicting a lower leg. The B refers to the Greek word *botanē* (field of grass), while the lower leg is supposed to be emblematic of the part of the dismembered Osiris that corresponds to the constellation of Aquarius. The keyword is Libas, a "spring or stream."

The twelfth field seems to be begun with a symbol of a cosmic egg, followed by the sign of the goddess Ananke, and the sign of the Egyptian flail, as seen in zone 3.3. Agrell identifies the keyword as Makros Kosmos, "the great order," which according to the Hermopolitan cosmogony arose out of an egg.

The first symbol in the thirteenth zone is problematic. It appears to be a demotic Egyptian sign. The second sign is the hieroglyph of a gravestone or stele, while the third figure is indicative of the threefold nature of Hekate. Her three names are Nychie ("Nocturnal"), Dione ("Goddess"), and Phoibie ("Inspired"). Agrell uses the name Nychie for the keyword of this zone.

Zone fourteen is begun with what appears to be the Greek letter *thēta*. This may refer to the name Thouros, the "Stormy one," as a way to denote the god Ares/Mars. The second symbol is interpreted by Agrell as an Egyptian "portable shrine," and the third symbol as an "open booth supported by a pole." Both of these structures are temples imitating the vault of heaven. The keyword is Xiphias, a "swordfish." This was the term used for a comet—which in ancient times was usually thought of as a portent of disaster.

The fifteenth zone contains three signs: one meaning "house," one meaning "throne," and one meaning "rainwater." The house is the "house of Helios (the Sun)"—in Greek, *oikia tou heliou*—whence the keyword of the zone: *oikia,* "house."

The first symbol in zone sixteen is that of river water. From this the keyword Potamos, "river," is derived. The second sign in the zone indicates two stars, which are often seen to the sides of depictions of Mithras. The third sign is thought by Agrell to be an abbreviated version of the symbol for the Egyptian god Set. The magical papyri (*PGM* V.5) indicates a unity of the gods Zeus-Helios-Sarapis-Mithras.

There has also been an altar found with an inscription dedicated to this combination of divinities. Sixteen is the number of Mithras, and he was especially honored on the sixteenth day of every month.

This ends the second ring or circle of zones on the Pergamon disk. The next, innermost, ring again reverses the order of reading and is to be interpreted in a clockwise direction as with the first ring.

Field seventeen, belonging to the letter *rho,* has three signs. Agrell interprets these as meaning "protection," from an Egyptian hieroglyph, the number 10,000 (in Egyptian notation), and a sign meaning "child." The keyword Agrell uses for this field is the name of the Egyptian goddess of childbirth, Renet, which relates the fact that a name (Egypt. *ren*) was given to the child upon birth.

The eighteenth zone, which corresponds to the letter *sigma,* also contains three symbols. The first of these is the three-pronged sign of Hekate. The second is interpreted as a "headrest," with reference to the god of dreams, Hermes. The third sign is again that of "fire" as seen in zone 4.2. To this zone Agrell ascribes the keyword Sthenno, the "goddess of fear."

Zone nineteen, corresponding to the letter *tau,* contains only two symbols. The first of these is a double *zēta* (ZZ) connected by a bar. According to the old magical numerology of the Greek stoicheia, *zēta* = 6. So a double *zēta* is a sign of twelve. This is seen as a reference to the twelve signs of the zodiac. The second sign in the field is interpreted by Agrell to be a stylized version of the Egyptian hieroglyph for the *ka,* or "soul." In Babylonian astral mythology, the body was ruled by the twelve signs of the zodiac, while the soul was ruled by the seven planets. The Greek keyword for this zone is Tarichos, the "embalmed body of a person."

The twentieth field apparently has a figure missing. This was probably obliterated due to damage to the metal. On the basis of comparative evidence, Agrell reconstructs the sign /\/\/\ for the Egyptian word *nw* [noo], "water." The Greek "N" as the second sign is phonetic confirmation of this reconstruction, as it indicates the sound with which the keyword begins in Egyptian. The third sign in the zone is an Osirian crook-scepter with the hieroglyph for "bringing." As Osiris is the god of the fields and plant growth, Agrell interprets this as "bringing the power and glory of Osiris" = water. The keyword in Greek fittingly is ὕδωρ (húdōr), "water."

Zone twenty-one, ascribed to the Greek letter *phi,* contains three signs. The first two serpentine shapes are mirror images of each other. Agrell attaches a phallic meaning to the snakes and makes the keyword of the zone Phallos. The first serpent is seen as a favorable sign; the second, a reversal and therefore unfavorable. The third sign is emblematic of the union between male and female.

The twenty-second field contains only two signs. The first appears to be a dwelling or booth with a pole in the middle. The second is unmistakably a crescent moon. The Greek keyword Agrell ascribed to the zone was Chrēma, meaning "goods" or "money." He also indicates the general belief that the Moon provided silver and was a source of good luck in financial affairs.

Zone twenty-three is ascribed to the Greek letter *psi.* This letter also appears to be doubled in a glyphlike form as the first sign in the zone. Agrell compares the shape of this sign with the bundle of lightning bolts carried by Zeus–Jupiter Dolichenus. He also notes that the shape of the letter *psi* (Ψ) may be the source of the astrological sign for Jupiter: ♃. The second sign is an Egyptian hieroglyph indicating that the querent must "bring sacrifice" as a punishment from the god to atone for some situation in life. The Greek keyword is either Psophos, "noise," or Psolos, an obscure word for "lightning."

The last of the twenty-four zones contains three signs. The first of these is the now familiar trifoil symbol for Hekate (as also seen in fields 10 and 18). The second sign appears to be a capital Greek *alpha,* which Agrell attaches here to the name Ἄιδης, Hades-Pluto, the giver of riches. In the Egyptian context this would be Osiris. The last sign is linked with the Egyptian numerical symbol for ten. Agrell assigns the keyword Opheleia, "help," to this zone. But it is perhaps better served with the name Ὧρος (hōros), "barrier," or "cosmic limit."

For a comparative overview of the twenty-four stoicheia and their relationship to other elements of the lore, see table 1 in appendix E on page 162.

Agrell perhaps overemphasized the value of the magic disk of Pergamon in determining the meanings of the Greek stoicheia and in discovering the original meanings of the tarot cards. It seems that there are links among the fields of the disk, the Greek stoicheia, and the Arcana, but they are indirect and approximate. However, conservative and careful use of this material can lead to important insights into the symbolic systems of the magical culture of the first few centuries CE.

The Northern Link

R emarkably, there indeed seem to be systemic links among the Greek stoicheia (as used in Mithraism), the Roman alphabet, the tarok, and the runes used by the ancient Germanic peoples. Germanic runes constitute a writing system of an alphabetic type—that is, each character represents a sound (phoneme) in the language. It is most probable that the runes originated some time during the last two centuries BCE. The oldest known runic inscription, found on the brooch of Meldorf, dates from the middle of the first century CE. As a general rule regarding the history of alphabets, the origin of a given system can be placed as much as two hundred years prior to the oldest known inscription. (This is because the earliest inscriptions tend to be on highly perishable objects often made of wood.)

Neither is it a meaningless coincidence that the word used to denote these symbols in the Germanic tongue, *rūnō,* or *rūna,* means first and foremost "secret," or "mystery." As noted in chapter 4 (page 72), this is the exact same meaning of the Latin word *arcanum* (pl. *arcana*). Both connote that the symbol called by this name both conceals information and reveals a mystery—for those initiated into their understanding.

The oldest form of the runic system is known as the Older Fuþark. It consists of twenty-four characters, or rune-staves. The system is usually named for the phonetic values of the first six runes: F-U-Þ-A-R-K. This system was in use for making inscriptions for divinatory, magical, and religious purposes from perhaps as early as 200 BCE until about 750 to 800 CE. Since this covers the time period we are interested in here, I do not need to go into the intricacies of runic history beyond this period.

The runes bear a close resemblance to certain features of both the Greek and Hebrew alphabetic traditions. Besides consisting of twenty-four characters, the Older Fuþark is also commonly divided into three groups of eight characters—just as were the Greek alphabeta of the period. But like the Hebrew letters, each of the rune-staves bears a special name, with a definite meaning in the Proto-Germanic language in which they were first encoded. Due to the fact that each rune belongs to a certain position in the row, each rune also has a numerical value.

It has already been mentioned that there was heavy Mithraic activity along the northern border of the Roman Empire in the first few centuries CE. Many members of the Mithraea certainly belonged to Germanic tribes from either side of the imperial borders. There is no reason to believe that syncretization between Mithraic and Germanic religious conceptions did not take place in these regions, just as it had in the Italic, Egyptian, or Middle Eastern regions.[1] In fact, there is strong graphic evidence for this. For example, in the Mithraeum at Dieburg in Germany there is a depiction of Mithras riding a horse and carrying a spear instead of being in his customary chariot armed with bow and arrow. This depiction is clearly one drawn from the image of Wodan, the magical god of the contemporary Germanic tribes of that region.

Moreover, many scholars of Germanic religion have noted the striking similarity between cosmological conceptions in the Norse Eddas and the traditions of the northern Iranian steppe peoples such as the Scythians and Sarmatians. The Parthians too had originally belonged to this culture before moving southward into more urbanized Persia. This could be due to a combination of common ancestral roots and later secondary influence of Iranian tribes (for example, the Sarmatians) on the migrating Germanic tribes from as early as 200 BCE to as late as 700 CE.

These historical facts led the Swedish scholar Sigurd Agrell to investigate the possible links between Mithraic tradition and that of the runes. This investigation concluded in his controversial Uthark theory, which states that the runes have their origin in Mithraic letter/number magic. It is called the Uthark theory because Agrell posited that the original order of the rune staves did not begin with the F-rune but with the U-rune.

This theory has been generally rejected by academic runologists for two reasons: (1) no runic artifact or primary runic document indicates anything but a F-U-Þ-A-R-K order, and (2) the runes must have originated in a time before the advent of Mithraic influence in Europe. However, it is possible that the Mithraic tradition informed, or reformed, the lore of the runes on a secondary level at a later date (during the first few centuries of the Christian era) and that this material was encoded in the runic tradition by means of a simple encoding device. This device, commonly used in magical and mystical operations involving alphabetic speculations, involves simply shifting the values of the letters by one. In this case the numerical code was shifted so that the first rune became the last, the second then became the first, and so on. This new, esoteric numerical order is reflected in columns IX–XII in table 1 on page 163. This possibility is strengthened by the evidence which Agrell's theory focuses on the question. When we look at the Mithraic values of the Greek stoicheia and the mythic values ascribed to them, and the exact order in which they occur, and we compare this series of twenty-four meanings with the sequence of runic values, the results are sometimes astounding. Indeed, many patterns seem too exact to be anything but intentional. But because this Mithraic connection is only revealed when the shift in numerical code is observed, it remains esoteric.

Neither can it go unremarked that in many instances it seems that Agrell used the runic tradition to fill in the gaps in the Mithraic and Hermetic lore. This is remarkable, since there is relatively more information of a general type about the southern and eastern cults and relatively little about those in the North. However, when it comes to lore about the runes versus lore about the Greek stoicheia, there is usually more specific and consistent information about the runes. This is mainly due to the existence of several "Rune Poems" in Old English and Old Norse, as well as numerous references to them in the Old Norse mythic corpus known as the *Poetic Edda*.

The most likely scenario for the secondary influence of the

Mithraic/Hermetic material in the runic tradition involves the wide-spread initiation of a number of Erulians into the Mithraic Mysteries along the Rhine and Danube Rivers between the fourth and fifth centuries. The Erulians were members of warrior bands known to have been knowledgeable of runes. Groups of these individuals would have then returned to the North after their retirement from military service and would have brought the knowledge gained through their Mithraic initiations with them. However, they clearly did not continue purely Mithraic practices in the North—but rather synthesized what they had learned into a seamless Odian whole.

An alternate scenario would have it that the stream of influence went much more in the opposite direction: that the Roman cult of Mithras (at least among the soldiers along the Rhine and Danube) was largely "Odinized" due to the influence of the initiated Erulian soldiers who joined the Mithraea and infused their runic knowledge into the lore of Mithraic practice.

In the former case, with Mithraic elements entering into the northern runic tradition, it could be that in the North we have the true continuation of the Mithraic initiatory tradition—which was effectively wiped out in the South by the growing power of the Catholic Church.

Without doubt there was prolonged and in-depth cultural exchange between the Germanic peoples and various Iranian steppe peoples from as early as 600 BCE, an exchange which become more intense after the first century CE and throughout the Migration Age.[2] Connections with the East remained strong even after Iran had become Islamic during the so-called Viking Age in the North. This was a time when what came to be known as the Eastern Road led directly to Iran, or what the Norse called Serkland ("Shirt-Land" or "Silk-Land"). Among the earliest contacts were those with the Sarmatians and Alans. Among the most famous runic artifacts are the spearheads of Dahmsdorf and Kovel, which are both inscribed with runes as well as a Sarmatian *tamgas,* or "tribal signs," along with other magical or religious symbols such as the crescent moon, swastika, and the triskelion.

Interactions with the Iranian tribes, some of which were

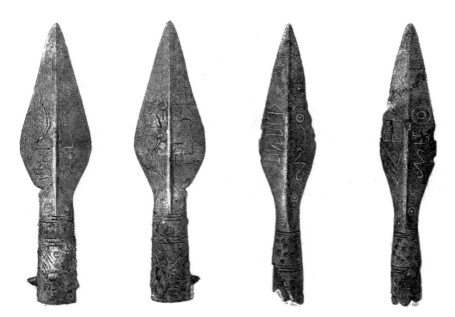

The Spearhead of Dahmsdorf (left); the Spearhead of Kovel (right)

Germanicized (some Germanic tribes were also absorbed into the Iranian ethnic groups) left definite imprints on the lore and mythology of the North. The contact with the Mithraic doctrines as taught by the Roman Mithraists would therefore have seemed very familiar to the Germanic soldiers, which would have only added to the popularity and prestige of those teachings among the latter.

For those primarily interested in the lore of the runes, the Iranian and Mithraic teachings offer useful building blocks for the restoration and reawakening of certain details of the tradition with recourse to material from purely pagan sources.

TABLES OF GREEK AND ROMAN KEYS TO THE TAROT

TABLE I. THE GREEK KEY (I–VI)					
I	II	III	IV	V	VI
Number	Greek Name	Value	Greek Keyword	Meaning of Keyword	Mithraic Meaning
1	alpha	1	Apis	cosmic bovine	Bull
2	beta	2	Bebon	a name of Typhon	the Demonic
3	gamma	3	Gnōsis	divine knowledge	the Divine
4	delta	4	Demeter	the goddess Demeter	Four Elements
5	epsilon	5	Edsên	double-headed lion (?)	Aion
6	zēta	7	Zemia	penalty	Sacrifice
7	ēta	8	Hedonē (ἡδονη)	pleasure	Joy/Love
8	thēta	9	Thalassa	sea	Crystal-Heaven
9	iota	10	Isis	the goddess Isis	Ananke
10	kappa	20	Kronos	the god Kronos	Kronos, Death
11	lambda	30	Libas	stream	Plants
12	mu	40	Makros Kosmos	great world (order)	Trees
13	nu	50	Nykie	nocturnal one	Hekate
14	i	60	Xiphias	swordfish (a comet)	Stars

TABLE I. THE GREEK KEY (VII–XII)

VII	VIII	IX	X	XI	XII
Arcanum (Esoteric Roman name)	Arcanum Number	Rune Shape	Runic Name	Translation of Runic Name	Esoteric Meaning of Runic Name
The Fool (Apis)	0	ᚾ	ūruz	aurochs	primal vital force
The Magician (Hacatus-Typhon)	I	ᚦ	þurisaz	giant	unconscious force
The Priestess (Caeles-Isis)	II	ᚠ	ansuz	the god	Wodan/Óðinn (divine consciousness)
The Empress (Diana)	III	ᚱ	raiðō	ride	vehicle/path of power
The Emperor (Ion-Aeon)	IV	ᚲ	kēnaz	torch	controlled energy
The Hierophant (Amen)	V	ᚷ	gebō	gift	sacrifice
The Lovers (Gaudium)	VI	ᚹ	wunjō	joy	ecstasy
The Chariot (Hamaxa)	VII	ᚺ	hagalaz	hail(-stone)	catastrophe
Justice (Iustitia)	VIII	ᚾ	naudiz	need	resistance/deliverance
The Hermit (Kronos)	IX	ᛁ	īsa	ice	constriction
Wheel of Fortune (Libera)	X	ᛃ	jēra	year	good harvest
Strength (Magnitudo)	XI	ᛇ	eihwaz	yew	tree of life/death
The Hanged Man (Noxa)	XII	ᛈ	perþrō	dice-cup*	force of "fate"
The Star (Stellae)	XVII	ᛉ	elhaz	elk	protective/tutelary numen

*made of pear (i.e., fruit-bearing) wood

TABLE I. THE GREEK KEY (I–VI) (continued)

I	II	III	IV	V	VI
Number	Greek Name	Value	Greek Keyword	Meaning of Keyword	Mithraic Meaning
15	omikron	70	Oikia	house (of Helios)	Sun
16	pi	80	Potamos	river	Serapis-Mithra
17	rho	100	Renet	the goddess Renet	the Feminine
18	igma	200	Sthenno	mighty	Bearer of Dea
19	tau	300	Tarichos	mummy	Human
20	upsilon	400	Húdōr (ὕδωρ)	water	Water
21	phi	500	Phallos	phallus	Phallus
22	chi	600	Chrēma	goods/money	Possessions
23	psi	700	Psolos	lightning	Zeus
24	omega	800	Opheleia	help	Riches

TABLE I. THE GREEK KEY (VII–XII) (continued)

VII	VIII	IX	X	XI	XII
Arcanum (Esoteric Roman name)	Arcanum Number	Rune Shape	Runic Name	Translation of Runic Name	Esoteric Meaning of Runic Name
The Sun (Victor-Unus)	XIX	ᚺ	sowilō	sun	crystallized light
The Devil (Quirinus)	XV	↑	teiwaz	Týr	sovereign order
The Moon (Trina)	XVIII	ᛒ	berkanō	Birch-Goddess	retainer/releaser
Death (Orcus)	XIII	ᛗ	ehwaz	horse	harnessed power
The World (Zodiacus)	XXI	ᛗ	mannaz	man	human order from divine ancestry
Temperance (Pluvia)	XIV	↑	laguz	water	life energy/organic growth
Judgment (Xiphias)	XX	◇	ingwaz	Earth-God	gestation (sower of "seed")
- ? -	-?-	ᛜ	ōþila	property	hereditary power
The Tower (Ruina)	XVI	ᛞ	dagaz	day	twilight/dawn
- ? -	-?-	ᚠ	fehu	cattle	wealth/dynamic power

TABLE II. THE ROMAN KEY

I	II	III	IV	V	VI	VII
Number	Letter Value	Esoteric Name	Translation of Esoteric Name	Tarot Arcanum	Arcanum Number	Esoteric Number Value*
1	A	Apis	Apis Bull	The Fool	0	1
2	B	Bacatus	Typhon	The Magician	I	2
3	C	Caeles-Isis	Heavenly	The Priestess	II	3
4	D	Diana	Diana	The Empress	III	4
5	E	Eon	Aeon	The Emperor	IV	5 or 8
6	F	Flamen	Priest	The Hierophant	V	80
7	G	Gaudium	Joy	The Lovers	VI	3
8	H	Hamaxa	Chariot	The Chariot	VII	8 or 5
9	I	Iustitia	Justice	Justice	VIII	10
10	K	Kronos	Time	Hermit	IX	20
11	L	Libera	Persephone	Wheel/Fortune	X	30
12	M	Magnitudo	Strength	Strength	XI	40
13	N	Noxa	Punishment	The Hanged Man	XII	50
14	O	Orcus	Death Realm	Death	XIII	70 or 80
15	P	Pluvia	Rain	Temperance	XIV	80
16	Q	Quirinus	Quirinus	The Devil	XV	100
17	R	Ruina	A Ruin	The Tower	XVI	100
18	S	Stellae	Stars	The Star	XVII	200
19	T	Trina	Threefold	The Moon	XVIII	300
20	V	Victor-Unus	Victor-One	The Sun	XIX	6
21	X	Xiphias	Swordfish	Judgment	XX	60
22	Z	Zodiacus	Zodiac	The World	XXI	7

*These number values have been adapted from the Greek and Hebrew systems and have been shown to work for esoteric Mithraic number symbolism. The Roman letter "Y," not used in the system of Arcana, has the esoteric number value of either 6 or 10.

GLOSSARY

HERMETICISM: Original Hermeticism is a loosely organized school of philosophy (and practical application of that philosophy) derived from Greek, Egyptian, Persian, Judaic, Chaldean, Gnostic, and Platonic and Neoplatonic ideas, which was first written down between the second and seventh centuries CE. This represents a syncretic system of thought that treads a middle ground between rationality and mysticism.

MAGIANISM/MAGIAN: These terms often generically refer to the priesthood (and the craft plied by that priesthood) that belonged to the Iranian peoples, especially those of the western part of the Persian Empire. These practitioners are generally thought to be a part of the Zoroastrian religion, but are not necessarily so, or not necessarily the most orthodox practitioners of the Good Religion. Often Magians are thought to be adherents of the Zurvanite form of Zoroastrianism prevalent during the time of the Parthian Empire (247 BCE–224 CE).

MITHRA: Avestan name of the Iranian god of contracts, justice, and god of the light of the sun, moon, and stars. He is the great intercessor. In ancient Iran he was the gateway to the divine realm.

MITHRAISM: This term designates the formal cult or Mysteries of the god Mithras, as practiced in the West during the time period of the Roman Empire.

MITHRAS: This is the Greco-Roman form of the name of the Iranian god Mithra. It is used in this book to differentiate the god of the

Hellenistic and Roman cults from that practiced entirely within an Iranian cultural context.

SAOSHYANT: An Avestan word meaning literally "one who brings benefit." In orthodox Zoroastrianism there is a doctrine concerning the coming of a world-savior who will usher in the transformation of the world into its original state of perfection and immortality. It is also thought that there will be several such figures in history whose activity will make the world better.

STOICHEION, PL. STOICHEIA: The Greek word used to denote a "letter" of the alphabet; the word also means "element."

TAROK: This is an alternate term for the "tarot," based on the Italian term *tarocco* and its possible connection with the piece of standard iconography of the Mithraic cult known as the tauroktonia.

YAZATA: A standard Avestan term meaning "one worthy of worship" used to designate the beneficial divine beings of Iranian mythology. In orthodox Zoroastrianism the term may be translated as either "god/dess" or "angel." They are often abstract principles that have been transformed into objects of cultic worship.

ZARATHUSTRA: A priest of the archaic Iranian religion who lived perhaps as early as 1700 BCE. He received a flash of insight that led him to realize that all gods were derived from one source, Ahura Mazda (Lord-Wisdom), which can best be described as pure focused consciousness. He set about the reform of religion on this basis and formed a Great Fellowship to hand on his words and philosophy.

ZOROASTRIANISM: This term is used to designate the orthodox religion founded by, and based upon the philosophy of, the early Iranian prophet Zarathustra.

ZURVANISM: A particular theological and philosophical stance with regard to the interpretation of Iranian, and specifically Zoroastrian, myth and religion. It postulates that Eternal Time is the ultimate level of reality from which everything subsequently sprang. Zurvan (or Zurvân) is an androgynous, neutral entity.

Notes

INTRODUCTION.
THE MAGIAN TAROT
AND POSTMODERN THEORY

1. Flowers, *Hermetic Magic,* 140. Punctuation slightly modified.

CHAPTER 1.
A MODERN HISTORY OF TAROT

1. Huson, *The Mystical Origins of the Tarot,* 25–28.

CHAPTER 2. MAGIANISM AND
MITHRISM/MITHRAISM

1. See Cumont, *The Mysteries of Mithras,* 132–38.
2. See Cumont, *The Mysteries of Mithras,* 116–18.
3. Cumont, *The Mysteries of Mithras,* 130.
4. Cumont, *The Mysteries of Mithras,* 107.
5. Cumont, *The Mysteries of Mithras,* 130–32.

CHAPTER 3. MAGIAN TEACHINGS
OF THE STOICHEIA

1. Cumont, *Oriental Religions in Roman Paganism,* 146.

CHAPTER 4. THE MAGIAN TAROK

1. Dumézil, *Archaic Roman Religion,* 409–10.
2. Dumézil, *Archaic Roman Religion,* 132.
3. See, for example, *PGM* VII.429–58.
4. Eliade, *A History of Religious Ideas,* vol. II, 314.
5. Eliade, *A History of Religious Ideas,* vol. I, 331–33.
6. Cumont, *The Mysteries of Mithras,* 146.
7. Agrell, *Die pergamenische Zauberscheibe und das Tarockspiel,* 159–60.

APPENDIX B. A GREEK ALPHABETIC ORACLE

1. For the entire ancient Greek text, see Heinevetter, *Würfel- und Buchstabenorakel in Griechenland und Kleinasien,* 35.

APPENDIX D. THE NORTHERN LINK

1. For a speculative consideration of the possible relationship between Germanic and Mithraic religious conceptions, see Kaliff and Sundqvist, "Odin and Mithras: Relgious Acculteration during the Roman Iron Age and the Migration Period," and the further bibliographic references provided there.
2. For more on this topic, see my essay "Germanic and Iranian Culture and Myth: Connections, Analogs, and Influences" in *TYR: Myth—Culture—Tradition* 5 (2018), 141–71.

BIBLIOGRAPHY

PRIMARY SOURCES

Bundahis. Translated by E. W. West. Sacred Books of the East, vol. 5. Oxford: Clarendon, 1880. Pp. 3–151.

The Greater Iranian Bundahishn. Edited by Zeke J. V. Kassock. Fredricksburg, Md.: Kassock Bros., 2013.

The Rig Veda. Trans. Ralph T. H. Griffith. Sacred Writings, vol. 5. New York: History Book Club, 1992.

The Greek Magical Papyri in Translation. Edited by Dieter Betz. Chicago: University of Chicago Press, 1986.

Papyri Graecae Magicae. Edited and translated by Karl Preisendanz. 2 vols. Stuttgart: Teubner, 1973–1974.

SECONDARY SOURCES

Agrell, Sigurd. *Die pergamenische Zauberscheibe und das Tarockspiel.* Lund: Almqvist & Wiksell, 1935–1936.

Boyce, Mary. *Zoroastrians: Their Religious Beliefs and Practices.* London: Routledge and Kegan Paul, 1979.

Clauss, Manfred. *The Roman Cult of Mithras: The God and his Mysteries.* Translated by R. Gordon. New York: Routledge, 2001.

Roberts, Richard, and Joseph Campbell. *Tarot Revelations.* N.p.: Richard Roberts, 1979.

Cumont, Franz. *Oriental Religions in Roman Paganism.* New York: Dover, 1956 [1911].

————. *The Mysteries of Mithras.* Translated by Thomas J. McCormack. New York: Dover, 1956 [1903].

Dornseiff, Franz. *Das Alphabet in Mystik und Magie.* Leipzig: Teubner, 1922.

Dumézil, Georges. *Archaic Roman Religion.* Translated by P. Krapp. 2 vols. Chicago: University of Chicago Press, 1970.

Eliade, Mircea. *History of Religious Ideas.* Translated by W. Trask, A. Hiltebeitel, and D. Apastolos-Cappadona. 3 vols. Chicago: University of Chicago Press, 1978–1985.

Flowers, Stephen E. *Hermetic Magic: The Postmodern Magical Papyrus of Abaris.* York Beach, Maine: Weiser, 1995.

————. *Original Magic.* Rochester, Vt.: Inner Traditions, 2017.

————. "Germanic and Iranian Culture and Myth: Connections, Analogs, and Influences." *TYR: Myth—Culture—Tradition* 5 (2018): 141–71.

Heinevetter, Franz. *Würfel- und Buchstabenorakel in Griechenland und Kleinasien.* Breslau: Barth & Co., 1912

Hornung, Erik. *The Secret Lore of Egypt: Its Impact on the West.* Ithaca, N.Y.: Cornell University Press, 2001.

Huson, Paul. *Mystical Origins of the Tarot: From Ancient Roots to Modern Usage.* Rochester, Vt.: Destiny, 2004.

Kaliff, Anders, and Olof Sundqvist. "Odin and Mithras: Religious Acculteration during the Roman Iron Age and the Migration Period." In *Old Norse Religion in Long-Term Perspectives: Origins, Changes, and Interactions,* edited by Anders Andrén, Kristina Jennbert, and Catharina Raudvere. Lund: Nordic Academic Press, 2006. Pp. 212–17.

Kaplan, Stuart. *Encyclopedia of the Tarot,* vol. I. Stamford, Conn.: U.S. Games, 1978.

Littleton, C. Scott. *The New Comparative Mythology.* Berkeley: University of California Press, 1973.

Lévi, Éliphas [Alphonse Louis Constant]. *Transcendental Magic.* Translated by A. E. Waite. London: Rider, 1896.

Lindsay, Jack. *The Origins of Alchemy in Greco-Roman Egypt.* London: Muller, 1970.

Luck, Georg. *Arcana Mundi: Magic and the Occult in the Greek and Roman Worlds.* Baltimore: Johns Hopkins University Press, 1985.

Machiavelli, Niccolo. *The Prince.* Translated by T. Bergin. Arlington Heights: Harlan Davidson, 1947.

Merkelbach, Reinhold. *Mithras.* Königstein: Hain, 1984.

Mirandola, Pico della. *Oration on the Dignity of Man*. Translated by Charles Glenn Wallis. Indianapolis: Bobbs-Merrill, 1940.

Moeller, Walter O. *The Mithraic Origins and Meanings of the Rotas-Sator Square*. Leiden: Brill, 1973.

Opsopaus, John. *The Oracles of Apollo: Practical Ancient Greek Divination for Today*. St. Paul, Minn.: Llewellyn, 2017.

Place, Robert M. *The Tarot: History, Symbolism, and Divination*. New York: Tarcher/Penguin, 2005.

Scholem, Gershom, ed. *Zohar: The Book of Splendor*. New York: Schocken, 1949.

———. *Kabbalah*. New York: Meridian, 1974.

———. *Origins of the Kabbalah*. Princeton: Princeton University Press, 1987.

Seznec, Jean. *The Survival of the Pagan Gods: The Mythological Tradition and Its Place in Renaissance Humanism and Art*. Translated by Barbara F. Sessions. New York: Harper and Row, 1953.

Smith, Morton. *Jesus the Magician*. San Francisco: Harper and Row, 1978.

Tegtmeier, Ralph. *Tarot: Geschichte eines Schicksalsspiels*. Cologne: Dumont, 1986.

Ulansey, David. *The Origins of the Mithraic Mysteries: Cosmology and Salvation in the Ancient World*. New York: Oxford University Press, 1989.

Waite, Arthur Edward. *The Pictorial Key to the Tarot, Being Fragments of a Secret Tradition under the Veil of Divination*. London: Rider & Son, 1911.

Waterfield, Robin, trans. *The Theology of Arithmetic*. Grand Rapids, Mich.: Phanes, 1988.

Widengren, Geo. *Die Religionen Irans*. Stuttgart: Kohlhammer, 1965.

INDEX

Page numbers in *italics* indicate tables and illustrations.

BOOKS OF RELATED INTEREST

Original Magic
The Rituals and Initiations of the Persian Magi
by Stephen E. Flowers, Ph.D.

Icelandic Magic
Practical Secrets of the Northern Grimoires
by Stephen E. Flowers, Ph.D.

Lords of the Left-Hand Path
Forbidden Practices and Spiritual Heresies
by Stephen E. Flowers, Ph.D.

The Fraternitas Saturni
History, Doctrine, and Rituals of the Magical Order
of the Brotherhood of Saturn
by Stephen E. Flowers, Ph.D.

The Secret of the Runes
Translated by Guido von List
Edited by Stephen E. Flowers, Ph.D.

Secret Practices of the Sufi Freemasons
The Islamic Teachings at the Heart of Alchemy
by Baron Rudolf von Sebottendorff
Translated by Stephen E. Flowers, Ph.D.

Infernal Geometry and the Left-Hand Path
The Magical System of the Nine Angles
by Toby Chappell
Foreword by Michael A. Aquino, Ph.D.
Afterword by Stephen E. Flowers, Ph.D.

The Way of Tarot
The Spiritual Teacher in the Cards
by Alejandro Jodorowsky and Marianne Costa

INNER TRADITIONS • BEAR & COMPANY
P.O. Box 388
Rochester, VT 05767
1-800-246-8648
www.InnerTraditions.com

Or contact your local bookseller